LETTER
to TROY

Echoes Of Redemption

DAVID CARINGER

LETTER TO TROY
Echoes Of Redemption
by DAVID CARINGER

Printed in the United States of America.

ISBN 9781498442787

Cover photo by Tech. Sgt. Erica Knight USAF

www.xulonpress.com

Table of Contents:

Acknowledgements vii
Forward ix
Introduction xi

Chapter 1   Reflective Correspondent 17
Chapter 2   Carefree Child 21
Chapter 3   Inquisitive Adolescent 46
Chapter 4   Soldier Novitiate 70
Chapter 5   Acrophobic Optimist 95
Chapter 6   Conflicted Patriot 123
Chapter 7   Recalcitrant Professional 155
Chapter 8   Subdued Sinner 181
Chapter 9   Lonely Reprobate 201
Chapter 10   Aging Rebel 235
Chapter 11   Explosively Redeemed 254
Chapter 12   Redemptive Echoes   277

Acknowledgements

First and foremost, I thank my King and Redeemer Jesus Christ. He is the only reason this story has any relevance or value. I am very thankful for my parents who taught me the truth and tirelessly prayed for me through all of my dark years with unrelenting fervor. I thank my wife, Patti, for standing by me with love and grace through this process and encouraging me to complete this project. I offer special thanks to Patti, Thelma, Susan and Wilma for their editing assistance. I thank my siblings, Dennis, Steven, and Susan for their contributions to my life as I was growing up. I thank God for my children, Catherine, Gregory, and Jennifer, my step-children, Nathan, Kelly, and Pamela, and for my eight grandchildren. All of them have added priceless meaning and memories to my life. I thank my pastors, John Lindell and Tim Keene, for planting God's Word in me so deeply that even I couldn't forget it. I thank the members of our Life Group which is a dynamic part of the James River house-church ministry. Our Life Group family has blessed us in more ways than I can possibly note here. I thank my employers, Ken and Contessa Stallings, for their patience and unwavering support. Ken, God has clearly used you and your incredible generosity to make this book possible. I thank my extended family at CoLiant Solutions. You are all wonderful to work with. Last, but certainly not least, I thank my dear friend Troy Jackson for giving me a reason to write this very long letter. May God richly bless you as you read it.

Foreword

G od is a storyteller. Redemptive history is a brilliant story. Scripture is filled with stories of God working in and through the lives of people. The stories of God's redemptive work are still being written in the lives of those who come to know Him. And, not only is God a storyteller, but He loves it when people tell the stories of what God has done in their lives to those around them. In Psalm 118:7, the Psalmist gives voice to a call that runs throughout the entire Bible when he writes, "I will proclaim what the LORD has done." We have been commissioned to tell the story of what God has done for us. One of the joys of being a pastor is hearing stories of life change and watching the effect of those stories ripple into the lives of others. Personal testimony possesses its own unique power. When someone tells their story, God's work in their life spills over into the lives of those who hear it. There is something about hearing someone tell his or her story that moves the heart in a way that the straightforward relay of information simply cannot. This is the power that lies within the pages of David Caringer's book, *Letter to Troy: Echoes of Redemption*. It is a story that embodies the biblical call to declare the works of God.

The pages of this book are filled with insights about life, relationships, and God's transforming grace. The potency of these insights is increased by the fact that David is living what he writes. While there is much to be gleaned in the chapters that follow, perhaps what is most stirring is the reminder of the power our testimony possesses and the delight God finds in His people telling the stories of what He has done.

John Lindell
Lead Pastor, James River Church

Introduction

I am greatly honored that my brother, David Caringer, has asked me to provide the introduction for his book. As I read the book, I contemplated all the things I've lost in my life and the grief of loss and joy of recovery I've experienced. Over the years, I've lost my keys, my phone, my wallet, important documents, my glasses, my car in the parking lot, and countless umbrellas, just to name a few items. I even lost my youngest daughter in a department store when she was five (only for a few minutes, but it seemed like eternity). The fact is, I'm very prone to distraction, and I've never developed a good system for taking note of where I put things before I walk away.

I realized as I listed all those temporarily or permanently missing treasures that the level of anxiety I feel upon losing them is directly correlated to their value. I become annoyed if I have to replace yet another umbrella. I become frantic if I can't find my keys or my glasses. I was literally paralyzed with fear when I couldn't find my daughter. Many times, in my panic of loss, I've prayed diligently that God would direct me to a missing item or help me retrace my steps and recall my actions to locate it.

There is an important lesson in this that I feel is the message of David's book. Jesus described in three stories the feelings of anxiety when something is lost. He also described the joy of recovery when the missing treasure is found. He used these stories to illustrate the awesome love of God. I can definitely relate to the parable of the lost coin found in Luke 15:8-10. How many times have I turned my home or office inside out in a frenzied search for an absent article in much the same way as depicted in Jesus story of the woman who lost this treasured coin? And, when I've found my missing treasure, I'm flooded with relief and want to celebrate just as she did. These coins were very valuable to this woman. No one coin was more valuable than another, however. Even though she had nine left, she could not rest until the last coin was safely in her possession.

Through the parable of the lost sheep recorded in Luke 15:4-7, Jesus portrayed the anxiety and joy of loss and recovery to his followers. This reminds me of the feelings I experienced when my daughter was lost in the store. He described the actions of a shepherd who had one hundred sheep. At the end of the day, ninety-nine sheep were safely accounted for and with the shepherd. However, there was one out there...one that was lost. As the shepherd counted his sheep and discovered there was one missing, his anxiety spurred him to action. Knowing that one last sheep was separated from the flock and from his protection, probably hurting and possibly in mortal danger, the shepherd would not rest.

He would leave the ninety-nine and comb the wilderness seeking the one that was lost.

To further emphasize God's love for us, Jesus related loss and recovery to a parent's experience as He spoke of a father with two sons. One son was obedient and stayed at home, but the other rebelliously defied his parents, demanded his inheritance and went off to a far country to party and live a degenerate lifestyle. Though he had one son still at home, the father greatly grieved for his lost son. When the rebellious son had spent all his money and was reduced to working as a pig farmer's helper, so hungry he was tempted to eat the pigs' food, he came to his senses. He could not imagine that he would be accepted back as a son in his father's house and planned to bargain for a servant's position. To his father, however, the lost son had never lost his value.

I can imagine this father looking out the window each day in the direction he had last seen his son. On the day the formerly rebellious son walked back down the road toward his home, the father probably thought he was dreaming. He may have rubbed his eyes and wondered, "Could it really be him?" He didn't wait for the son to make it all the way to the gate. He ran to him and threw his arms around him. The son was filthy, in rags, and smelled of a lifestyle the father detested, but he threw his arms around him and welcomed him home with great joy.

"But while he was still a long way off, his father saw him and felt compassion, and ran and embraced him and kissed him. And the son said to him, 'Father, I have sinned against heaven and before

you. I am no longer worthy to be called your son.'
But the father said to his servants, 'Bring quickly
the best robe, and put it on him, and put a ring on
his hand, and shoes on his feet. And bring the fat-
tened calf and kill it, and let us eat and celebrate.
For this my son was dead, and is alive again; he
was lost, and is found.' And they began to celebrate" (Luke 15: 20-24).*

Jesus compared the celebration of found treasure
from each story to the celebration in heaven when a
soul who is lost turns to God. For the celebration of the
found coin, he stated, "Just so, I tell you, there is joy
before the angels of God over one sinner who repents"
(Luke 15:10b). Relating to the recovery of the lost sheep,
he affirmed, "Just so, I tell you, there will be more joy
in heaven over one sinner who repents than over ninety-nine righteous persons who need no repentance"
(Luke 15:7b). What I found most important about these
stories was that Jesus was telling us how valuable we
are to God. No matter what we've done or where we
are, God is diligently seeking us out. He doesn't tire of
finding us, and he has the power to set circumstances in
motion to lead us to him. When we come to our senses
and come to God as the rebellious son did to his father,
we don't have to be perfect. We can be filthy and carrying the stench of our sin, but it doesn't matter to God.
We're still valuable to him.

That's what David's story is all about. It's about rebellion, loss, and recovery. It's about God being faithful
when we are not. It's about the great joy of discovering
that, no matter what we've done or where we've been,

when we feel worthless and are viewed as worthless by others around us, we are immensely valuable to God. Jesus said we can count on that. God's love is unconditional and His desire for relationship with us is unfathomable. David's life has illustrated that, and I'm proud of him for the honesty with which he has told his story. His great desire is that you see God's great love through this book. David's telling of his story at times made me laugh. At other times, it made me very sad. So much time was wasted and so much damage was done.

However, there was great joy when he came to God, in our family and in heaven. God has redeemed what was lost and made David's life better than it has ever been. If you are lost and desperate for change, it's no accident that you have picked up this book to read. God is seeking you. The grief felt by men and women when we lose a treasure is what God is feeling for you magnified immeasurably. Unlike a man or woman who has lost something, God has the power to set events in motion for those who are lost to find Him. This is how He seeks us out. Nothing you've done is a surprise or hidden from Him, and yet He loves you and wants relationship with you. You're not too far away, and you haven't done too many bad things. Just as God took David's shattered life and put the pieces back together into something greater than David could have imagined, He can do the same for you. He can bring you the peace you long for through the completeness of relationship with Him.

Dr. Susan Caringer Langston, Ed.D.
Associate Professor of Education, Evangel University

Chapter 1

Reflective Correspondent

"So now faith, hope, and love abide, these three;
but the greatest of these is love."
(I Corinthians 13:13)

Troy, You and I have spent many long hours discussing the big issues regarding life on planet earth. We haven't always agreed, but we've always consented to disagree with peace and mutual respect. I believe you know this, however it's worth repeating; I'm honored to have you as my friend and brother in Christ. I decided to write this letter in an effort to share and better explain some simple truths that I've come to know through what may seem like a strange collection of experiences and a "never too late" study of God's Word.

It seems a peculiar fact that people so often find themselves embroiled in odd circumstances almost as if coincidentally. It's not at all uncommon for a person to become involved in the greatest of adventures or disasters without really stopping to consider how or why. I no longer believe in accidents. I firmly believe that everything happens for a reason.

The Bible teaches that every event, no matter how seemingly dramatic or inconsequential, is part of The Creator's sovereign plan. Skeptics have wrongly accused God for a very long time claiming He can't be truly "good" because He allows bad things to happen to "good" people. This theory simply illustrates the ignorance of the skeptics. These people are trying to understand the plan of God through their limited human intellect and perspective.

A critical flaw in the skeptics' claim is the idea that "good" people are harmed by the "bad" things that are allowed to happen. As a practical matter, there is a difference between "good" and "innocent". There are really no "good" people because all humans inherit the sin nature which has been passed from generation to generation since the fall of man in the Garden of Eden. Human infants are innocent because they have not yet reached the age of accountability. They are not yet able to choose between right and wrong. Innocence is based on inability to exercise choice. The inherited sin nature dictates that children choose rebellion as soon as they are able to make a choice. They can no longer be considered innocent after that. They are, in fact, enslaved by the sin nature passed down to them from their fallen ancestors.

Innocent babies are protected by the awesome grace of God. Guilty sinners are redeemed through that same awesome grace. Innocent children and redeemed adults do, tragically of course, suffer harm and loss. Tragedy is part of life in our fallen world because evil entered the world through man's rebellion. The Creator's Master Plan has been at work ever since to repair the damage done and restore God's creation to perfection. This plan will be fulfilled. All the tragedies wrongly attributed to God will ultimately "work together for good for those who love God and are called to His purposes".

I've experienced the beauty and majesty of God's creation in my life. I've also done and experienced a great many evil things. Sadly, I've both inflicted and suffered tremendous harm. I've enjoyed many grand adventures, but I've endured an even greater number of self inflicted tragedies. When God saved me, He saved me from my own absurd pattern of bad choices. He reconciled me to Himself by giving me access through Jesus to His awesome grace as a matter of His perfect choice. He relentlessly kept calling me until I finally gave up and surrendered. It was His effort that saved me, not something that I did or didn't do on my own.

I know our personal backgrounds are very different Troy. I understand that our families have different cultural and political views. Regardless of these differences, I know we share many of the same basic values. We've been taught right from wrong; we value truth, justice, peace, and true Biblical love; we want our children and their children to live in prosperity and safety; we want them to surrender their lives to Jesus and become mighty men and women of the living God. We do have differences, but I believe we have even more in common. I know we are in complete agreement regarding the basic appreciative values of love, faith, hope, and courage.

19

These values affect our success or failure in every human endeavor.

The Apostle Paul wrote four letters to the struggling church at Corinth. Two of these letters are included in the New Testament. Paul gave a detailed explanation of the magnificent spiritual gifts in 1st Corinthians and encouraged the church to seek the greatest of these gifts. He then pointed out that without love; none of these gifts had any real value. Paul went on to explain what true love really is and taught that all the listed spiritual gifts would pass away in time. Only faith, hope, and love will endure. He adamantly declared that love is the greatest of these three remaining virtues. I add courage to my list because I believe it is a foundational element of all three of these primary virtues.

I've finally come to understand that we are saved by God's grace through faith in the awesome gift of Jesus Christ. There is nothing we can do to earn it. There is nothing we can do to keep it. It is absolutely free to us, but to God, it came at the highest price ever paid. This gift of salvation provides us with a future and hope. We live out our salvation by expressing our faith through love. I didn't always understand this. I spent many years living as an enemy of God and His Kingdom. God never gave up on me even in the darkest days of my rebellion. When I finally reached the end of myself, He was there. When I finally surrendered everything to Him in a desperate cry for mercy, He blessed me with something far better. Perhaps, the best way to explain what I'm trying to say is to tell you my personal story...

Chapter 2

Carefree Child

*"When I was a child, I thought like a child, I reasoned
like a child. When I became a man,
I gave up childish ways."*
(I Corinthians 13:11)

I was born into a solidly fundamental protestant
Christian family in Chicago in the late 1950s. My father
was a Nazarene minister, but he stepped away from
active vocational ministry when my parents began to
have children. My mother was and is one of the sweetest
church ladies I've ever known. She was a stay-at-home
mom most of the time while we were growing up.

My birth certificate says that I was born on May 9,
1957. However, my birth date is actually a little more
complicated than that. My parents were conservative
republicans. Daylight Savings Time (DST) was adopted by
the federal government during World War II as a means
of allowing a longer work day without added concern

for the necessary blackout conditions in coastal cities. The federal government at that time was mainly controlled by the democrats. Many people in the US, especially republicans, thought temporary wartime measures such as DST would end when the war ended. The fact that these laws continued long after the war was a surprise to many people.

One of the nurses in the maternity ward (during the foggy groggy hours after I was born) was busy filling out my birth certificate. For some inexplicable reason, the nurse asked mom if she wanted to use Standard Time or DST when recording the time of my birth. Mom, ever the solid republican, considered that DST was still a temporary political manipulation which would someday disappear. She selected Standard Time. My time of birth was officially recorded as 11:58PM on May 9, rather than 12:58AM on May 10. Sometimes, I feel like I've been conflicted ever since.

I have two older brothers and one younger sister. Our dad, a giant of a man physically, intellectually, and spiritually, owned a small trucking company in Chicago during our early childhood. He was greatly respected by everyone who knew him and had a well earned reputation for always being trustworthy. Mom and dad taught us right from wrong. They didn't rely on the church or school to handle that important responsibility without their input and direct personal influence. They taught us to exercise the courage to love God, to stand up for what is right, to defend the helpless, to love our country, and to love our fellow man. Dad was the one who first taught me that courage is not the absence of fear. He taught me that real courage involves controlling or conquering our fear and doing what is right.

Our neighborhood in the early 1960s was diverse, but the families did what they could to help each other. The children in the neighborhood usually did most things together. The neighborhood moms worked together to watch over and protect each other's children. Chicago was a dangerous place, even back then, but the collective society of that time taught children to obey their parents and to respect authority. It was not unusual for a disobedient or rebellious child to receive a well deserved swat or two administered by a teacher or school principal. The parents usually sided with the teacher and discipline was enhanced when the child went home and told his parents that he had been spanked at school. I also remember late summer evenings when you could hear the voices of neighborhood moms calling their children home for supper. It wasn't unusual for these ladies to include the names of another family's children when calling their own children home if the flock of kids had strayed too far.

We prayed in public school when I was a child, even though the practice was essentially outlawed in 1963 by a foolish Supreme Court decision. We also stood up and recited the pledge of allegiance to the flag with our right hands over our hearts. You were only considered different or weird if you didn't participate. We were taught in school that America was great because the national motto "In God We Trust" was true; we were taught that America was great because America was the most powerful and most generous country on earth. We were taught that America was free; that our freedom was purchased with the blood of our heroes; and that freedom was good. We were taught that America was exceptional. We were also taught the value of a hard day's work. Our parents (all of our parents) had survived the great depression. They taught us it was better to save our money, so we would have enough to buy what we needed, rather than foolishly spend our money on things that were not necessary. We didn't always listen, but they taught those lessons diligently because they loved us and we knew it.

We were aware of racial inequality and segregation in the Chicago of the 1960s. However, these evils were mostly thought of as a scourge of the Deep-South. Our community was a mixture of different cultures. Our blue collar neighborhoods were naturally merit success oriented. People either carried their weight or they didn't. They were judged mainly on merit not on the color of their skin. The civil rights movement led by Dr. Martin Luther King, Jr. and others was something we viewed from a distance. That didn't excuse our parents and our leaders from a responsibility to speak out for what was right, but the cancer-like plague of institutionalized racial bigotry was something that had existed in the Deep-South since well before the Civil War. To be sure, there was racial bigotry in the north. However, when I was a child, racism was commonly recognized in the north as morally wrong. A racist was a racist no matter what race he or she belonged to. Racism wasn't normally part of our public life in the north back then. We didn't think much about it; we got along with those around us or we didn't. When we didn't get along, we were correctly labeled as obnoxious or antisocial.

Most of the dads in the 1960s were veterans of either WWII or the Korean conflict. Our dad was too young to be involved with most of WWII, although several of his brothers served in the US Navy. Dad tried to join the navy in early 1945 at age 17, but was turned down because he was color blind. He ended up joining the US Merchant Marine Service instead. He served as a cook on a Liberty ship that was transporting troops back and forth from Europe during the closing days of the war.

Our parents met in St. Louis when he was sixteen and she was fifteen. He had left home to escape his abusive father and was staying with his older brother. She lived at home with her parents and two sisters. They married after dad was discharged from the Merchant Marine Service and mom graduated high school. Mom's twin sister Wilma left home after high school to attend Olivet Nazarene College in Kankakee, Illinois. She met and married Arland (Al) Gould not long after she started college. Uncle Al was an older man (in his mid-twenties) who had a profound influence on dad. He was a WWII veteran who was studying to be a minister. Dad finished high school at Olivet. He then attended two years of college to become a licensed Nazarene minister along with Uncle Al. The two couples shared living quarters during this time. Dad supported himself and mom by driving a truck when he wasn't studying.

Dad was, before anything else, a man of God. He was impeccably honest. He kept his promises or he renegotiated in an open and outright manner. We didn't have to wonder whether we could trust him. We just knew. He was extremely intelligent. Dad never obtained a formal education above an associate's degree, but he read constantly and had an incredible memory. He knew more about the Bible and a wide range of other subjects than most of the people near him at any given time. He wasn't arrogant about it though. He genuinely cared about those around him. Dad wasn't perfect, and he did have a sharp temper at times. His physical size and booming voice made him a commanding physical presence. He also had a strong sense of humor and a quick tendency to laugh at himself when appropriate. He would usually only display frustration or anger when he observed that someone was hurting themselves or others that he cared about.

Dad had the heart of a pastor, and that made him a great leader and teacher. He was astute and quick-witted enough in business to make the right choices most of the time. He bounced back quickly if he made a mistake and pragmatically put the past behind him. Dad loved mom. Everyone around them understood this. They were married for life. The quickest way to bring my father into mortal combat would have been to threaten or show disrespect toward my mother.

Mom took care of all the details of daily life. She cooked, cleaned, taught, sewed, barbered, mowed, organized, nursed, doctored, painted, fixed, and otherwise "handled" every large or small project that presented itself. She raised four children while maintaining our household, managing the business bookkeeping, and actively participating in church events. Through all of that, she kept her sense of humor and maintained a humble dignity that never wavered. A pretty accurate description of mom is easily found in Proverbs, Chapter 31.

Our family lived in Chicago until I was in the third grade. Dad owned a small trucking company with several trucks and a small group of drivers. They mostly hauled chemicals and heating oil. Dad had some trouble with the local teamsters union when one of his drivers destroyed a company truck through abject negligence. Dad let the man go but was forced to rehire him by the union. The obvious unfairness of this situation had to have weighed very heavily on my father.

The company obtained a very difficult contract to haul aircraft de-icer onto Midway airport soon after this incident. This was during a brutally cold winter. I remember dad working almost around the clock for days on end and only sleeping for short periods of time before going back to work again. He began experiencing physical difficulties and eventually sought medical treatment. The doctors told him that he had severe hypertension and cardio vascular disease. At age thirty four, he was told that he would not live until he was forty. His response was that if he was going to die, he wanted to die where it was warm.

Dad had an older brother, Uncle Lonnie, who lived in Southern California. I remember dad asking us if we would like to have a family vacation in California. We excitedly said yes and soon embarked on one of those legendary family road trips down US Highway 66. We spent a couple of weeks in Highland, California visiting with family. We went to the beach for the first time and visited places like Disneyland and Knott's Berry Farm. Our experience in what seemed like paradise was sadly soon over. We reluctantly started the long drive back to the cold and ice of the upper Midwest.

Dad decided to take the more northern route which took us through Las Vegas, Nevada on our way back to Illinois. We were in a new Pontiac station wagon. The passenger arrangement for our family involved me and my two brothers riding in the back seat, mom in the front passenger seat, and dad driving the car. My little sister always sat on the front seat between my parents. I'm not saying that child seats didn't exist in those days, but if they did, no one knew what they were.

Las Vegas at that time was not the sprawling metropolis it is now. There were not many hotels and casinos on the strip. The hotels that were there seemed to simply stick up out of the desert in what appeared to be near the middle of nowhere. Dad looked over at mom that day, as we approached the city, and announced his intention to show his children the evils of gambling. Mom suggested that this was a very bad plan. He insisted it was an excellent idea, and he had already made up his mind.

Dad drove into town and parked the car in the lot of a large casino hotel. Mom elected to stay in the air-conditioned car with the engine running while dad got out and led his four children into the front doors of the casino. We must have looked like the proverbial mice following the Pied Piper. No one stopped or questioned us when we got inside. Dad pointed to a row of slot machines arranged along the wall to the left. He stepped over in front of one of these machines and explained how it worked. He followed this technical explanation with a forceful lecture about a fool and his money being swiftly parted. He produced a coin and again explained how quickly people threw their money away. Inserting the coin in the slot and cranking the handle with dramatic flair, he showed us how the money was now gone.

Dad produced another coin and inserted it into the machine as if to reinforce the lesson. Cranking the handle as he smiled at his children, he must have felt like he had demonstrated a very solid object lesson for us. The machine registered triple 7s this time, unfortunately, and mechanically announced a huge jackpot win. Bells began ringing and lights began flashing. Change was spraying out of the dispenser on the machine and coins were rolling all over the floor. My brothers and I did what any normal boy would do in this situation. We dove for the money and began cramming it into our pockets. My little sister was screaming with delight.

A very fit looking young man in a dark business suit approached us at about this time. The man spoke sharply to dad telling him to get his children out of the casino. We swiftly gathered up the scattered change and went back out the same front doors we had entered. We marched back to where mom was patiently waiting in the parking lot. My two brothers and I had bulging pockets and a stony faced appreciation for dad's object lesson on the evils of gambling. My little sister was probably experiencing similar emotions, but she didn't have any pockets. Dad opened the car door for my sister to climb in, and mom asked what had happened. Dad just said, "Don't ask", and we quietly resumed our family road trip. My brothers and I spent that change all the way to Tulsa.

Our parents sold the business and our family home when we got back to Chicago. Dad purchased a used moving truck and we moved to Highland, California, in February of 1965. Dad completely changed his vocation.

He got a job as a salesman at an American Motors dealership in San Bernardino. Mom went to work as a bookkeeper for a shoe company during this time.

Everything was different for us in California. The culture was as alien in our minds as the climate. There were orange groves everywhere in those days. The country was beautiful, but smog was a terrible problem most of the time. School was different. The people were different. Everything seemed to be a lot more relaxed than it was in Chicago. We moved into a new house a block away from Uncle Lonnie and his family. Our cousins, Jessie and Ricky, looked very much like my brothers and me. There was no doubt in anyone's mind that we were related.

My parents quickly got involved in a local church where dad often served as a lay pastor. Our family participated in church events at almost every opportunity including Sunday school, Sunday morning and evening services, Wednesday evening prayer meetings, youth group meetings, vacation bible school, pot-luck dinners, picnics, youth camp, and many other activities. The church was our family's center of social contact. We had friends at school, and I'm sure our parents had friends at work, but our closest friends and acquaintances were in the local church. It seemed like our family was in church every time the doors were open even if they were just cleaning the place up.

Our family adapted to the Southern California lifestyle over the next few years. The culture was even more diverse than that of Chicago. By the time we moved, the Civil Rights movement had made great strides in the Deep-South. America was becoming increasingly entrenched in what was now referred to as the war in

Vietnam. Our new home in Highland, California was very close to Norton Air Force Base. Norton was a critical logistic base for material being shipped to and from Southeast Asia. As the war intensified, the air traffic in and out of Norton also intensified.

Smog was a new experience for us. I remember days when the wind would shift in such a way that the smog from the Los Angeles metro area would collect in the San Bernardino valley so thickly that we would get smog warnings. We would be advised not to go outside unless it was absolutely necessary. The itching and burning in your bronchial tubes let you know that the air was indeed poisonous if you breathed deeply during these times.

We learned about the citrus industry, the gold rush, and earthquakes at school. We learned to ride skateboards and to build wooden, down-hill go-carts out of old lumber and lawn mower wheels at home. I think I may have narrowly escaped a tragic end on more than one occasion while riding one of these go-carts down the steep residential streets and trying to stop by using a primitive wooden stick brake. I know now that God was watching over and protecting me and my siblings.

Our parents had an in-ground swimming pool installed in our back yard the year we moved into our new house. The novelty of swimming year round was great. We had all been taught to swim when we were very young. We soon spent so much time in the water that our hair started to develop a weird greenish tint from the pool chemicals. We were curious children, and we began to experiment with all kinds of stuff in the pool. Most of these things were relatively safe. However, some of the experiments my brothers and I tried in that swimming pool were dangerous, and a few were really reckless.

We had been watching scuba divers on television one day when we decided that there should be some way for us to spend more time underwater than what was possible with a single breath of air. My oldest brother and I eventually figured out how to float underwater with neutral buoyancy by tying two large plastic pool chemical boxes together. The box on top was separated from the one on the bottom by about two feet. The top box was turned upside down, and the bottom box was filled with large rocks. Both boxes were placed in the water so that the entire contraption submerged. The air trapped in the top box would make it float. Changing the number of rocks in the bottom box would make it either rise or sink. We were able to take quick breaths from the stale air in the top box and stay under water longer than we might have otherwise. Yes, this was foolish and dangerous. Again, God was protecting us, and no one was injured.

Mom and dad were both working very hard outside the home at this time. My oldest brother was in his mid teens. Our parents relied on him to look after us when we were at home and they were at work. This arrangement may seem strange today, but back then there was nothing unusual about an older sibling serving as baby sitter to younger brothers and sisters. Our nautical adventures were always pursued when mom wasn't home. The scuba experiments were ended abruptly one day when she came home early.

Mom had an older model vacuum cleaner that was shaped amazingly like a small wheeled torpedo. The suction hose attached to the front, the collection bag was stationed in the center, and the exhaust air was ejected from the back. We somehow discovered that you could remove the suction hose from the front and attach it to the back. If you connected the hose this way, air was blown out through it when you turned the vacuum cleaner on. If you removed the dirt collection bag, the air was more or less dust free.

We were filled with dubious and lopsided determination to emulate our frog-man, scuba-diving heroes on TV. We took the vacuum cleaner out to the back yard one day. We rearranged the hose, removed the collection bag, and plugged the machine into an exterior wall outlet near the side of the pool. We dropped the hose under the water and dove in after turning the vacuum cleaner on. The fact that we were not immediately boiled in high voltage seems amazing now. We had been under water for several minutes taking breaths as needed from the hose when we heard a strange screaming noise reverberating through the water. We looked up through the surface in time to see the distorted image of our dear mother as she ran to unplug her misused household appliance before her children managed to electrocute themselves. We were banned from scuba for the foreseeable future.

My brother Steven and I spent a great deal of time with our cousins Ricky and Jessie and became very close. We got involved in Cub Scouts, then Webelos, and later Boy Scouts. We played Little League Baseball. We rode everywhere in town on our bicycles and no one thought anything about it. If we were not at school or church, we spent most of our time outside. We thought we were being punished if we were required to stay inside during good weather. It still seems incredibly odd when I see children inside their homes playing video games or watching television on beautiful days. We went out and sought adventure. As I've already explained, we spent a great deal of time swimming. We also built tree houses and make-shift forts, played hide and seek, hiked in the surrounding foothills, and raced go-carts. Before we left the house on summer mornings, mom made us do a short list of chores. We did these as quickly as possible and then headed out to conquer the unknown. When we had to come inside in the evening, we were usually exhausted but full of plans for the next day's adventures.

I was quite a bit smaller than many of the other kids my age during elementary school. I was told by my siblings that I was stubborn, obnoxious, and bull-headed. These attributes helped lead me into a peculiar learning experience when I was in sixth grade. There was a young man in my class who was larger than most of the other boys. He had unfortunately taken advantage of his size to become an insufferable bully. One day during lunch recess, a great number of us had congregated at the end of the playground quite a distance from the school buildings. The bully selected me to torment that day and confronted me in the middle of a sizeable group of my friends. When I didn't respond as he wished to his taunting, he took a swing at my head with a wild round-house punch. I ducked, and the blow missed. This made him even angrier. He stepped forward and slugged me low and hard in the stomach. I was bent over in furious agony.

The bell rang signaling the end of the lunch period at that moment. All of the other children, including the bully, began running toward the school. Tears were nearly blinding me, and I felt an overwhelming sense of indignant rage. In a moment of vindictive fury, I reached down, picked up a golf-ball size stone, and looked up to see my tormentor running toward the building about twenty yards away. Strengthened by adrenalin in the moment, I heaved the stone into the sky aimed generally in the bully's direction. Much to my surprise, the timing and trajectory of the missile were nearly perfect. A pro quarterback like Archie Manning or Joe Namath would have been proud. The bully literally ran up under the stone as it came back down and impacted directly on his head. He dropped like he had been shot.

All of my friends started cheering. I had struck a blow for the down-trodden. We all ran past the prostrate form of the now humbled tyrant and went on in to class without even considering any type of first aid. I was sitting in Mr. Munson's sixth grade class trying to learn something about thirty minutes later when I heard my name announced on the public address system. I was told to report to the principal's office immediately. I saw the bully sitting on a chair near the wall crying when I went into the outer office as I remember. He had a white bandage wrapped around his head with a blood spot on it. He bore a striking resemblance to the wounded fifer in the old color guard paintings from the Revolutionary War. The receptionist told me the principal was waiting for me and I was to go right into his office.

The school principal was a dignified elderly gray-haired gentleman who always seemed to be dressed in a dark suit, with a white shirt and tie. He was sitting behind his desk with the air of a High Court Judge preparing to render a verdict. He got directly to the point when he saw me come in and asked for my side of the story. I was still angry, but I was also pretty scared of the august majesty behind the desk. I sucked up my courage and told him about being bullied. I told him about being humiliated and punched. I told him about the inspiration to throw the rock. I also did my best to explain that the rock actually managed to hit the bully through some kind of freak accident.

The principal seemed understandably skeptical with regard to my accident theory, but he didn't leap over the desk and start thrashing me with the legendary "board of education". He scolded me about taking the law into my own hands. I was amazed when he went on to say he understood my reaction to the bully. He then uttered words that ruined my whole day. He had decided to send me home with a note. I was to give the note to my father and have him sign it. The principal told me I couldn't come back to school without the signed note.

This incident happened on Friday at the start of an extra long weekend. We were to have at least four days off from school as I recall. I rode my bicycle home from school that afternoon thinking long and hard about what I should do with the cursed note. I knew dad would decree some severe punishment that would put a damper on the long weekend if I gave him the note as instructed. I couldn't get back into school if I didn't give it to him though. I reasoned and rationalized until I was finally convinced that the best thing to do was to tear up the note and throw it away. I pedaled a few hundred feet on toward home after doing this before suddenly realizing how stupid this was. I turned around and went back to get the note. I hurried on home after gathering up the torn pieces. It was frighteningly clear that I was in even worse trouble now because I had torn the note up. I climbed up in the garage attic rafters when I got home and hid the note between one of the rafter beams and the wall. No one would ever look there. This seemed like it would give me time to think and decide what to do.

Dad announced that we were not going to spend our long weekend in idleness that evening at supper. He wanted us to do some important chores around the house. The first of these chores was to clean up the garage. This was to include cleaning out the garage attic. My brothers found my torn up note the next morning. They saw that I was terrified, and they decided to use the note to extort extra work from me. I was soon doing a lot more than they were. This went on until Sunday morning.

Dad was sitting at the breakfast table that morning waiting for the rest of us to get ready for church. My brothers continued to torment me over the note and demanded that I polish their shoes. This was the straw that broke the camel's back. I suddenly couldn't stand the injustice any longer. I marched into the dining room and got my father's attention. He put down his paper and turned to me. I took a deep breath and blurted out everything that had happened. I'm not sure what was going through his mind. He had a strange look on his face as I finished my confession. The next thing I knew, my brothers were both getting the punishment I had expected. Mom and I carefully taped the note back together and dad signed it. He gave me a stern lecture about where I had strayed, and told me that he thought I had already been punished enough. He asked mom to take me and the note to the principal's office when school resumed, and the incident was more or less forgotten. The bully never again picked on me or anyone else I knew as far as I can remember.

My oldest brother Dennis began to grow away from his younger siblings at about the same time he learned to drive. He was adjusting to high school and starting to date. We didn't understand much of that. He just seemed to be distant. I looked up to him as a hero. We still did some things together, but the relationship was definitely changing. I was sitting in our living room watching cartoons on television one Saturday morning because it was overcast and a little cold outside. Dennis had planned for a date to come over to our house that afternoon and swim in the backyard pool. It was really too cool outside for this, but the pool was equipped with a gas water heater.

I remember Dennis walking out the sliding glass door that separated the living room from the back yard patio area. He was wearing a brown corduroy jacket. I distractedly watched as he walked around the swimming pool to the large metal enclosure that housed the pool water heater. He opened the panel on the near side of the box and bent down to turn the system on. He then stood up abruptly. He snapped his fingers in frustration and began walking back toward the house. He slid open the glass doors abruptly, stormed into the kitchen, and began rummaging through cabinet drawers. He went back past me through the living room and out to the swimming pool heater again a few minutes later.

I could easily see much of what Dennis was doing from where I was sitting as I tried to pay attention to the cartoon on TV. He reached the box and bent down to continue lighting the gas pilot for the heater. I realized he was trying to strike a match, when suddenly he was engulfed in a great ball of fire. The explosion was instantly extinguished. My brother spun toward me with a painfully shocked look on his face. His eyebrows were smoking and so was the front of his corduroy jacket. He let out a startled shriek and jumped directly into the ice cold pool water. He had turned on the gas without the pilot light. The gas had built up inside the box while he was in the house looking for matches. The explosion should have seriously injured or killed him. I believe God was protecting all of us. There was no pool date that day. Dennis insisted on wearing his baseball cap to school for the next week or so while his eyebrows grew back.

Most of the kids in our neighborhood practically lived on their bicycles. This was our primary means of transportation. My brother Steven began to experiment with riding on the firebreaks and mountain paths of the foothills surrounding our neighborhood. It was not at all uncommon for my brother to come home with his bicycle broken and his body looking like it had been dragged through a mesquite bush. He would get a strange gleam in his eyes when he got involved in any activity involving high speed.

I remember one afternoon when he came home telling me that he and his friends had found a great new hill where the path went almost straight down the mountain and then twisted violently back up and out of the way. They had begun calling this stretch of the path "dead man's hill." This treacherous section of mountain trail seemed to offer an appealing satisfaction for my brother's growing addiction to speed. He was practically carrying his broken bicycle and excitedly asked to borrow mine. I turned him down. He "borrowed" my sister's bike instead without taking the time to ask her. My sister had a yellow bicycle with a white flowered basket on the front handle bars. I wasn't there to witness the event, but I can imagine what it must have looked like to my brother's friends when he came screaming down "dead man's hill" on that yellow flowered bike.

Dad soon introduced us to motorcycles with the purchase of a small street bike. As soon as we were taught how to operate it, we immediately started riding it on those same firebreaks and mountain trails. I learned to use a manual transmission without burning up the clutch on that little motorcycle. I had a small trail bike of my own within a few months. One of my oldest brother's friends borrowed my motorcycle one day and had an unfortunate accident in which the crank case was cracked and all of the oil drained out. He continued to run the engine not realizing what had happened. The motor was ruined and now appeared to be worthless. However, I was already developing some business skill at this point, and I traded this damaged motorcycle for an old mini bike. It had been in a garage fire and the seat was burned off, but the motor still ran and the tires were pretty good.

Dad found and purchased an old metal go-cart frame a few months later. We transferred the engine from the mini bike to the go-cart and I was back in motorized business. There was a dirt jogging track in a large field across the street from our house. I spent many long hours in great clouds of dust on that track. I raced around in that go-cart imagining myself to be a great race car driver like Al Unser or Mario Andretti. I had a very powerful imagination.

Books became one of my first addictions as soon as I learned to read. This only involved simple children's books at first. I was reading any adventure novel I could find by the time I was in fifth grade. Most of my childhood adventures were based on my effort to live out what I was reading in books. I read a book in sixth grade that told the true account of a paratrooper who had survived the campaigns in North Africa, Sicily, and Europe during WWII. I had already made up my mind that I wanted to be a soldier when I grew up. I was childishly fascinated with the idea of someday being one of those heroic paratroopers. My imagination was strong, but it was not yet able to add the awful terror, carnage, and depravity involved in war. The actual life expectancy of a paratrooper in combat was beyond my ability to comprehend. I was also unaware of my own looming fear of heights. I decided to become an infantry paratrooper in the 82nd Airborne Division when I finished reading this book.

I was saved at least 397 times, by my own conservative estimate, between the ages of eleven and seventeen. This was not true of course, but it accurately reflected the total misunderstanding that I had regarding the awesome grace of God and the wonderful gift of Jesus Christ. I believed that you were saved when you trusted in Jesus and asked Him to take your sins away. However, I also believed you had blown it and were no longer acceptable to God if you sinned in any way after that.

Our family attended church services whenever they were available as I've already explained. This included revival meetings. I would sit and listen to the preachers as they told of hell fire and damnation for lost sinners with this flawed theology at work in my young mind. It always seemed as if they were talking directly to me. I would respond to the altar calls and go crying to the front of the church where I would whole-heartedly pour out my sin and ask again for forgiveness and salvation. I would inevitably get caught up in some sinful behavior within a few days and suddenly realize (according to my distorted theology) that all bets were now off and I was again lost.

It wasn't until many years later that I finally learned the truth about God's grace. It eventually took years of study and many long hours of prayer and counseling with solid and mature fellow believers before I was able to fully accept what the Bible so clearly teaches. We are saved through faith by grace which was purchased at the highest price ever paid by Jesus Christ on the Roman cross at Calvary. We can't earn salvation by being good enough. There is nothing we can do to keep it. I now understand that there are really only two types of people in the world; the saved, and the unsaved.

I clearly didn't understand salvation when I was a kid. It was easy for me to believe that my parents were saved, or that the preacher and Sunday school teachers were saved. Me, however? I figured I was pretty much doomed. This confusion often led to a fatalistic approach to decision making. It may have resulted in my being a less well-behaved child than I would have been if I had known for sure that there was any real hope for my lost soul.

It was in this mindset that Steven and I swiped a pie from the church pot-luck dinner table one Sunday afternoon. All of the adults were engaged in some other activity in another area of the church. We went around behind the kitchen area and sat down against the back wall. After devouring the whole pie between us, we took the empty plate back in and returned it to the table. We thought we had cunningly put one over on our parents and the other adults in our church. Much to our dismay, we soon found ourselves forced by the social circumstances to eat a large pot-luck supper without showing any signs of being full to the point that we were about to burst. We knew it was wrong to steal. Our resulting stomach aches served as effective punishment for this mean-spirited act. Our shared misery should have taught us that our parents were really trying to protect us rather than deprive us.

Steven and I worked our way through the Scouting program until we were old enough to graduate from Cub Scouts and Webelos to become what we considered "real Scouts". In Boy Scouts, we started to participate in camping and hiking adventures unlike anything we had ever experienced. I loved being outside. I loved hiking out on forest trails to reach far away campsites. We would sleep in tents we had carried on our backs and eat food we had carried in our packs. I loved cooking outside over an open fire. I loved the clean mountain air. I was hooked.

We hiked up Mt. San Jacinto from near Idyllwild, California on one occasion. We planned to go all the way to the top of the mountain. We would then ride the tram down from the top to Palm Springs which is located at the base of the mountain on that side. The trip would take three days. We camped near the snow line on the first night. After we cooked and ate our suppers, each campfire was surrounded by several anxious scouts as the scout masters told us scary stories. These stories were designed to get us to stay in our pup tents after lights-out and not go wandering off into trouble.

We were told to clean our cooking utensils and pack our gear to prepare for the next leg of our hike the next morning. My brother either didn't hear the instructions or just didn't follow them. The scout master went to each boy and inspected our mess kits to make sure we had cleaned everything well enough to keep us from getting sick. Steven and another boy failed the inspection. They hadn't cleaned their pans or utensils at all. The scout master first decreed that they would immediately clean the equipment for reinspection. They would then have to "run a gauntlet" as punishment. I was horrified and angry. The punishment didn't fit the crime in my mind. All the boys in the troop would have to stand on either side of the gauntlet and strike the miscreants as they ran through. I couldn't get out of standing in the line, but I refused to strike my brother as he ran past. I went to Steven with tears in my eyes to try and console him when the humiliating event was over. I wanted to help him with his kit and let him know that I felt the punishment wasn't fair. Steven looked up at me with cold fury in his eyes as I approached. He had mistaken my intentions. He thought I had whole-heartedly participated in the gauntlet. He punched me straight in the nose as soon as I got close and began to speak. It wasn't until much later that I was able to explain to him what had happened.

Dramatic events like this only dampened our spirits for a short while at that age. The whole troop was involved in a massive snowball fight in the forest on the side of the mountain within a few hours. We eventually made it to the top and spent the night there before taking the beautiful tram ride down to the valley below. We learned a lot in scouting. It wasn't all about camping and roughing it in the wild.

Chapter 3

Inquisitive Adolescent

"For all have sinned and fall short of the glory of God."
(Romans 3:23)

My oldest brother had begun to get into a little trouble by 1969. Society had changed greatly since the 1950's. The drug culture was rampant in Southern California. Dennis had some run-ins with the authorities. I believe my parents attributed most of these problems to the social environment in California. The hippy movement was in full swing at that time. The sexual revolution seemed to have established headquarters in California. Long hair was not only in vogue; it was a badge of the resistance that fit the rebellious trend of the times. Rock and roll music had taken a drug culture turn to the left and was dragging the country's youth culture along with it. Marijuana was popular, but there was growing experimentation among young people with even more powerful illicit drugs like LSD, heroin, and cocaine.

Young American men were dying in droves in the jungles and rice paddies of Vietnam and there didn't seem to be any possible end in sight. We watched news footage of actual battlefield carnage in Vietnam with appalled fascination almost every evening. This war was not like the heroic events of WWII that we had learned about from our parents and history teachers. It seemed like some kind of monstrous meat grinder. The United States government had decided to maintain a position or presence in the conflict without actually trying to win it for political reasons that are astounding even to this day. There was no exit strategy. Through valiant bloody effort (that people at home would never fully appreciate) our troops would seize strategic objectives and hold them at great cost for a day or two. They would then be ordered to withdraw and concede the field to the otherwise vanquished enemy.

Our military forces could have won the Vietnam Conflict outright and ended it quickly, but they were not allowed to win. Our government had somehow inexplicably decided to string the war out in a bizarre contest of macabre attrition with the misguided hope that the communist government in North Vietnam would someday simply give up the fight from exhaustion. Our parents filled in a lot of the details for us almost unintentionally as they discussed the absurdity of the situation. I didn't need a great deal of explanation to understand these problems even as a child. I believe this is when I became a political conservative.

The news wasn't only full of tragic stories about Vietnam. There were a great number of other things happening at the same time. The civil rights movement had made great strides toward desegregation even in the Deep South, but there was still racial conflict. Racial tensions in the United States continued to rage throughout the 1960s, especially after Dr. Martin Luther King, Jr. was assassinated on April 4, 1968.

The space race was also in full motion. The Soviet Union became the first country to launch a functional man-made satellite into earth orbit with their Sputnik program in October, 1957. This was a shocking development to the United States which suddenly fell behind in the race. The Soviets also managed to send the first human into space in April of 1961 when Yuri Gagarin made this voyage aboard the Vostok 1 spacecraft. In response, John Glenn became the first NASA astronaut to orbit the earth aboard the Friendship 7 as part of the United States Mercury Program in February, 1962. We watched with fascination over the years as NASA went through the Mercury and Gemini programs pushing to beat the Soviets to the next big prize. Great strides were made, and in the late 1960s, NASA's Apollo program made all of us aware that soon, man really could reach the moon as promised by President Kennedy in 1960. It seemed highly likely we were going to beat the Soviets to it. That made it seem even sweeter.

This sweetness was more than simple nationalistic pride. Political and military competition between the U.S. and the Soviet Union had reached a dangerous level that threatened annihilation of the world as we knew it. The United States had been the first country to develop and use nuclear weapons. By the late 1950s, the Soviet Union also had them. The resulting conflict for ideological and political domination quickly grew into a global war of words, espionage, and threats. This was backed by an ever present fear of destructive forces that were difficult to comprehend. The term "Cold War" does not fully describe this period of world history. This war was very hot and violent in many parts of the world over a period of five decades. The United States and the Soviet Union came very close to mutual annihilation in what later became known as the Cuban missile crisis of 1960. God simply didn't allow it. The "conflicts" in Korea and Vietnam were essentially large campaigns of the Cold War. Hundreds of smaller battles and campaigns raged worldwide throughout the second half of the twentieth century. Rapid developments in engineering and science were usually tied very closely to military needs and weapons development. News of scientific achievements and events was usually delivered right alongside news regarding "wars and rumors of wars" from all over the world.

Many astounding developments occurred in space exploration, air travel, nuclear power, computer technology, and weapons systems throughout the decade of the 1960s. I watched TV in amazement as a twelve year old boy in 1969 when Neil Armstrong made his "one small step for man and one giant leap for mankind". The growing drug culture back on earth at this time was luring young people to make dangerous trips of a far more sinister kind without ever leaving the planet. Southern California seemed like "ground zero" to mom and dad for many of these events. This was just an illusion. The same stuff was happening all over the country. God in His amazing grace protected us through all of these dramatic changes.

Our parents decided that it would be best for all of their children if we were to move to a less progressive part of the country. Our maternal grandparents, and a large portion of mom's family, lived in and around Bolivar, Missouri. Dad had worked his way up through the hierarchy of the American Motors dealership in San Bernardino to the position of vice president and general manager. Our parents had worked very hard to reach a place where they were fairly well off and would have been considered upper middle class economically. They decided to leave all that behind and move to Missouri where they believed we would be protected from the worst of the ongoing social upheaval. They purchased a forty acre farm located on Piper Creek about five miles northeast of Bolivar. We made this move in the middle of my seventh grade year.

The culture shock for me and my siblings was dramatic. We must have looked as strange to the kids at our new schools as they did to us when we showed up on our first day. We had long sun bleached blond hair and talked with funny California overlaid Chicago accents. We didn't understand any more about hay hauling and animal husbandry than they did about tie-dyed T-shirts and body surfing. Even the music was different. These differences inevitably created friction and resulted in at least a few fistfights. I had long since gotten over the boyhood dislike of girls and developed a very strong appreciation for the female half of society. The country girls at the Bolivar Junior High School took a keen interest in the new boys with the strange city ways. The country boys also took an interest, but it was a violent one. I didn't feel accepted by my peers until the summer between seventh and eighth grade.

Life on the farm was great. It was sort of like going to camp without the usual camp limitations or agenda. We bought several small calves and bottle fed them until they could fend for themselves. My oldest brother Dennis bought a beautiful Tennessee Walker mare. I eventually bought a bone-headed Welch pony, and my sister Susan got a Shetland pony. We learned to hunt and fish. We learned to take care of the animals. We played in the snow in the winter and swam in Piper Creek during the summer. We built log rafts, camped in the woods, and had an all around great time.

Our maternal grandfather spent a great deal of time with us and taught us all kinds of things about living in the country and life in general. He showed us how to gig fish and frogs, how to trap small animals, how to clean game, and how to use an axe. At one point, grandpa decided that he wanted to have a cow that could give milk. We went to a farm auction where he purchased a Hereford cow with a very young bull calf. We subsequently learned how to milk and were fascinated to watch as mom churned some of the cream into butter.

Grandpa was a baseball nut. He loved the game. Our grandparents and their children moved to the St. Louis area during the Great Depression where Grandpa Berry found employment in heavy industry. He was an incurable St. Louis Cardinals fan. He loved to go to the games but couldn't afford to buy tickets. He eventually had a great idea that made extra money for his family and allowed him to see the ball games free. He became a hotdog vendor at the ball park and almost never missed another game. It wasn't uncommon to find grandpa asleep on the couch later in his life with a transistor radio propped up against his ear blasting the play-by-play of an afternoon Cardinal's game.

Grandpa decided to establish a large garden on the property after we had lived on the farm for several months. He let my brothers and I know that we were going to cut all the fence posts for this huge garden spot from the hardwood trees located on the farm. The fence posts were to be cut from hedge apple trees. The corner posts were to be cut from black locust trees. Both of these tree varieties might as well be made of iron if you plan to chop them down and convert them to fence posts with an axe rather than a chain saw. It took what seemed like months. We grew calluses on our calluses and blisters on top of those. I suspected at the time that the reason grandpa didn't want us to use a chain saw to cut those fence posts was because he was afraid of chainsaws or just thought they were too expensive. I now realize that he may have seen the possibility of developing us into power hitters on the local pony-league baseball team through the torturous exercise we endured while swinging that axe. The work didn't hurt us, whatever his reasons, and those days hold some of my fondest memories.

Grandpa taught us how to dig holes and set the posts when we finally got them all cut. He then taught us how to string the barbed wire. We learned how to plow, plant, hoe, and hope. We planted a lot of different things in that big garden. Everything grew very well at first. Unfortunately, there was a serious drought that year. The normal rainfall did not happen. Most of the crops didn't survive. This garden was huge. We had no effective way of fully irrigating it. Most of the plants burned up. We were only able to salvage a lot of green beans and some tomatoes. Mom canned most of the green beans. We were still going through those canned green beans almost a year later.

I was working on something in the back yard one afternoon and noticed my older brother entering the adjacent barnyard on his horse. He was riding the horse without a saddle. We often rode that way, especially in the summer. He had apparently been watching westerns on TV or something, because he had a coiled rope in his left hand along with the reins. Grandpa's bull calf was several months old now and it had grown a great deal since he purchased it along with the cow at the auction. My brother had one end of the rope tied around his waist. With coil and reins in his left hand and a loose "lariat" type loop in his right, he cantered the horse through the cow pies and debris that littered the barn yard as if he was looking for a victim.

I was intrigued by what I was seeing, so I stopped to watch. Seeing the unsuspecting bull calf walking through the lot from the other direction, my brother kicked the horse into higher speed and headed toward this irresistible target. As he passed the calf, he leaned over and threw the lariat over its head. This spooked the calf and it started to run in the opposite direction. The sound of the calf running spooked the horse and she began to gallop. My brother soon discovered he had a limited amount of rope. I know it was an optical illusion, but when the rope ran out, it seemed like my brother was suddenly, momentarily, suspended in mid air. The next thing I knew, he was skiing on his backside through the barnyard. I don't know how it ended. I was laughing too hard. As I recall he just disappeared in the distance while yelling and struggling to get loose. Of course, the louder he yelled the more the calf was spooked.

I got involved in school football when I was in eighth grade. I loved it although I was never very good at it. During practice one afternoon, I got my left little finger tied up in the cleats of another player and essentially broke the end of the finger off just beyond the last joint. Only a small piece of skin and fiber was holding the finger together. The doctor inserted a steel pin all the way through the joint to hold the bone together until it could heal. Although I have had worse injuries since, this was the most painful experience that I can remember. The reason I mention this, is that I believe it may provide a life lesson. This injury involved the smallest finger on my left hand. I am right handed. It doesn't seem like it should have been as important as it was to me. The pain was so excruciating however, that during my recovery, this small finger became the most important part of my body. I've observed that there are often small things in life that have the ability to change everything. Whether it's a spoken word, a simple gift, or a seemingly inconsequential act, small things can and often do have tremendous impact on our lives. Anyway, I haven't experienced physical pain like this from any other injury.

My brother Dennis graduated from Bolivar High School in 1970 and started life on his own. At the end of my eighth grade year, my parents made the decision to move back to Southern California. Dad's former employer in San Bernardino wanted him back. We packed up and moved to Yucaipa, California right after school was out that spring. We were soon deeply involved in the same church we had been attending when we lived in Highland. Dad was back at his old job with a promotion that gave him responsibility for two dealerships rather than just one. He still had heart disease, but by God's grace, his health had greatly improved. The Chicago doctors had been proven wrong about his expected early death. When the new school year started, I found myself enrolled in ninth grade at Yucaipa High School.

I finally started to grow physically and was able to make the ninth grade football team. The school at Yucaipa, California, was significantly larger than the one in Bolivar, Missouri. There were more than seven hundred kids in my ninth grade class. The entire student body of Bolivar High School was smaller than five hundred. We had been in Missouri just long enough to cause culture shock again when we returned to the Southern California environment. We made friends quickly back Then. Unfortunately, I also found out that I made enemies rather easily.

A huge crowd of students was waiting for the school busses to arrive one day when I was confronted by two of my classmates. One of these young men was clearly trying to push the other one into a fight with me. I think the animosity had started on the football practice field. The boy that was instigating the confrontation was not on the team, but the other one was. This one seemed to be slow and easily influenced by his friend. He was slightly shorter than me, but he was strongly built. I was scared, but I had been through similar incidents in the past.

The young man stepped forward and said something hateful to me at his friend's suggestion. He followed this up with a shove. The crowd of students seemed to sense something was going on and parted to make an open space near some wall lockers. I asked my assailant what his problem was. He answered by shoving me again. I knew where this was headed and didn't want to go there. I understood, by this time, that the best way to end a fight you didn't want and didn't start was to win it quickly. I struck my assailant as hard as I could on his left cheekbone with my right fist when he straightened up from the second shove. He stepped back and looked a little startled, then lunged forward slamming me against the lockers. I twisted out of his grasp. I punched him again as hard as I could in the exact same spot when he turned back to face me. I asked him to let it go and walk away. He refused and lunged at me again. Pushing off, I punched him again in the same spot on his left cheekbone. This went on for several minutes. I don't know how many times I punched this young man in the same place on his face. He finally realized that he was in trouble. I could see the look of anger in his eyes turn to fear. I didn't want to strike him again and he clearly didn't want to pursue his challenge any further. He finally gave it up and walked away. The buses showed up and I rode home with my brother Steven telling me to keep my head up when I was throwing punches in a fight.

It amazed me then that no teachers or school officials were aware of what was going on. No one intervened or tried to stop this fight. Granted, there were hundreds of kids in the area when it happened. The crowd was huge and the noise was almost deafening. It still seemed like something could have been done to prevent this kind of thing from happening. His friend just drifted away into the crowd like the coward that he seemed to be when my attacker decided to end the fight. His face was still swollen and discolored when the young man returned to school a couple of days later. I was glad I had won the fight, but I was also ashamed that I had done this to him. I felt like crying when I saw him. Maybe this was a rite of passage moment, maybe not, I'm not sure. I'm glad this kind of event became rare for me as I continued to grow physically.

Steven and I had started working to earn extra money in any job we could find. I worked the summer before school started that year at a local poultry farm. We both worked on Saturday's during the school year at one of the car dealerships that our dad was managing. We would spend the whole day cleaning and detailing the new cars that had been delivered to the lot before they were put out on display. By working hard and saving most of what I earned, I managed to build up enough money to purchase an old used dirt bike. Steven purchased a small street bike.

We decided to ride Steven's motorcycle up to Big Bear Lake and back one afternoon. It took a long while to get up there from where we lived. We couldn't find any reason for staying, so we decided to coast the bike down the mountain on the freeway. We started into one of the most harrowing experiences of my young life to that point with him on the front and me on the back of that motorcycle. I don't know how fast we were travelling with the engine off and the transmission in neutral, but I knew at the time that this was very dangerous and so did he. I also remember the view of the valley gorge far below us as we swept around the curves on this winding mountain highway and came very close to the embankment edge several times.

Our speed must have been close to one hundred miles per hour at different points of this ride. The trip seemed to take a long time regardless of how fast we were traveling. A lesson was delivered to both of us when we finally reached the valley floor. My brother was wearing the only helmet we owned, and it offered no face protection. I was bare headed. We had just survived the terror ride of our lives when a bee or wasp flew into the side of the helmet and started stinging Steven on the side of his head. He almost did wreck the bike when that started. We made it to the shoulder and survived the rest of the trip home. Steven was fifteen years old and I was fourteen on the day we made this ride. I know God was protecting us from our own foolishness.

My knowledge of God's grace was still as weak and confused as it had always been. This theological misunderstanding later made it possible for me to rationalize the first time I ever drank alcohol. I was in ninth grade at the time, and I was with the preacher's kids from the Nazarene Church we were attending. We had gone camping together. Both of these boys were doing everything they personally could do to live up to the negative reputation which is often attached to preachers' kids. I became quite intoxicated drinking with them that evening. I was violently sick the next day. Between the hangover and the solid realization that I had really blown it now, I cried out to God for forgiveness and made vows to never do anything like this again. Worse, of course, was yet to come.

I spent a lot of time in the weight room at the gym during the rest of the school year in Yucaipa. The head football coach seemed to see more potential in me than I saw in myself. I believe he was trying to develop me as a potential player on his team for the following year. I did gain a lot of upper body strength and weight that would help me in later endeavors, but we moved back to Missouri at the end of that school year. Dad had finally had enough of the rat race in California. He decided he would start his own used car dealership in Missouri. Our parents again sold their California home and purchased a new house in Bolivar. The used car dealership was soon in operation with financing from one of the local banks. Our family was again involved in the more simple country lifestyle of a small town in southwest Missouri.

I decided that I wanted to go riding in the country on my dirt bike one Sunday not long after we moved back to Missouri. It was a very warm summer day. My parents had given me strict instructions not to ride the motorcycle that day for some reason. I decided that I would go for a ride anyway while they were enjoying a well deserved afternoon nap. I pushed the cycle down the street a short way before starting it. I wasn't wearing a helmet. I never wore a helmet. I saw that the new highway was still closed and barricaded with highway department saw-horses as I neared the edge of town. I wasn't planning to enter the highway. I just wanted to go across to the dirt road on the other side.

I didn't notice that the saw-horses had been moved apart to open one lane. I didn't hear disaster approaching.

I had the wind in my face and the sun on my shoulder. Everything was great. I didn't notice the 1962 Chevy Impala approaching at almost 100 miles per hour. The driver was out drag racing on the newly completed, but still closed, highway. I turned my head slightly toward the noise when I did finally hear something. I believe the driver of the car finally saw me approaching the open space between the saw horses at about that same instant. He locked his brakes and the car began to skid. I had almost cleared the spot when the left front side of the car struck the rear wheel of the motorcycle from the left. The impact was directly behind the seat. The back of the motorcycle essentially disintegrated into the grill and headlight assembly of the car.

I don't remember much of anything else that happened for a while after that. I believe I kind of "came-to" a couple of times over the next hour. I do still remember some brief moments when people were talking to me almost as if it was part of a bad dream. I finally regained complete consciousness at St. John's Medical Center in Springfield, Missouri, many hours later. I had a skull fracture, a third degree burn on my right arm, and numerous cuts and bruises. This accident should have been fatal. Again, God was protecting me even in my disobedience. I can only imagine the anguish that I put my parents through that day. Mom and dad refused to allow the driver of the car to repair or replace my motorcycle because they rightly understood that, in order to gain a valuable life lesson, I needed to associate great personal loss with my rebellious action in this incident.

I had become so driven by the pursuit of girls between ninth and tenth grade that nothing else seemed to motivate me. I remember thinking that sex must be the primary motivator for everyone. It certainly was for me. Our parents had taught their children the facts of life when we were pretty young. This wasn't something I would willingly discuss with my parents by the time I got into high school. Suffice to say, I started early and had several very serious relationships during this time in my life. I did things that I should not have done without regard for God's marriage plan and way before I was ready to deal with any consequences.

I was drinking heavily and frequently at this time. It wasn't hard to find a party on Friday and Saturday nights. I knew what I was doing was wrong, but I believed myself to be lost anyway. My grades in school were barely strong enough to allow me to advance from one level to the next. I didn't like school. The only thing I did like about it was the opportunity to play football and chase the girls. The only classes that I really took an interest in during my junior and senior years in high school were history, shop, and sports. I did also enjoy my senior year French class, but this was only because the French teacher was a beautiful recent college graduate that had me and every other young man in the classroom trapped in a hope-less crush.

I worked after school and during weekends all the way through high school. Friday and Saturday nights were usually spent at ball games, parties, or out on dates. The local drive-in movie theater was a favorite haunt for me and most of my friends in school. It was not at all uncommon for several kids to be carried into the the-ater in the trunks of their friend's cars. The owners of the drive-in could probably have been more aggressive in preventing this piracy, but they likely made more on purchases at the concession stand than they did on tickets for admission. The back two rows of the theater were almost always filled with cars and kids that were only there for the party. I don't think many of us ever actually watched the movies being presented on the giant drive-in screen.

We also did a lot of "cruising" on Friday and Saturday nights. This old ritual involved hundreds of cars moving very slowly up and down a set of streets in virtually every city, town, and village in North America. These cars were always occupied by teenage kids with nothing better to do and not enough sense to realize the utter futility of their activity. Loud rock and roll music blasting from every one of these vehicles was mandatory for the cruise. This was also the era of the muscle car. Many of these cars sounded like they belonged on the drag strip or NASCAR track rather than a city street. It must have been miserable for anyone who lived anywhere near these streets. The sound was almost deafening to us most of the time. I understand why "cruising" is no longer legal in most communities.

The kids in the small town of Bolivar had a portion of State Highway TT measured to allow a quarter mile run at any speed achievable with plenty of room to slow down. This stretch of road was on the edge of town near the drive-in movie theater. It was far away from the center of town where the local police were focusing on the kids mindlessly cruising up and down between the town square and the Mr. Swiss drive-in restaurant. With the police otherwise occupied, anyone who wanted to try his skill and "need for speed" could and often did drag race out there.

These races were usually simple tests of ability, nerve, and muscle car strength. Sometimes they involved money, and it wasn't completely unheard of for the winner to have a claim on the loser's car title. I avoided these races because I had other things to do and I never had a car that could actually compete. I'm pretty sure that my brother Steven did participate. From what I heard, he was pretty good. Speed was just something that he did.

Tenth grade was pretty much the same as the last year had been. I was on the junior varsity football team when school started. I continued to work in any jobs I could find. I had just gotten my first driver's license when summer finally came. I bought an old Buick station wagon from dad's used car lot and went to work for a local brick layer carrying bricks and mixing mud. I helped build some houses that summer and worked on the masonry portion of a new church building. I also continued to grow more distant from the standards my parents had so lovingly set for their children. I didn't want to disappoint them. I just couldn't seem to avoid following the path I was on. I underwent the normal hazing and initiation process that was so common from high school upperclassmen in those days. I didn't at all like it, but I learned to endure it.

I went to work at a small local supermarket during the summer between tenth and eleventh grade. I kept this job until I finished high school. The store was owned by Delton and Lucretia Wade, the uncle and aunt of one of my best friends at school. Delton was a very dignified middle aged gentleman who always wore dark slacks with a white shirt and black bowtie under a crisp green apron while he was at work. This was the uniform he required all of his male employees to wear while we were in the store. Lucretia was a large and intense woman who ran the bookkeeping part of the operation with an iron will. Delton required an honest day's work for an honest day's wage. I learned a great deal about responsibility and reward from him during my employment there.

I worked almost every weekday evening after school until the store closed, and all day on Saturdays. The store was open on Sundays, but it closed early. I often worked on Sunday afternoons when needed. We had finished our cleanup duties and were preparing to close on one particular Sunday afternoon. I was in the back stockroom with a fellow employee named Tom. We were killing time and getting ready to go home. There were almost no customers in the store and the only other employees at work were two young ladies working the front registers. Time dragged. Tom and I began throwing a knife that was used for trimming produce into a wooden wall plank. We were more or less taking turns throwing the knife trying to come as close as we could to the target spot we had picked out on the plank.

We suddenly heard one of the ladies from the front registers calling over the PA system requesting customer assistance for a grocery carryout. I had the knife in my hand. Tom said he would go up front to help the customer. I said "OK. I'll come with you". I took one last throw at the plank as I started to follow. The knife sailed straight into a copper freon gas pipe that served the walk-in produce cooler. The blade sank into the pipe and stuck there. The gas had already begun to escape, and I made it worse in my panic by grabbing the knife and yanking it out. We tried everything we could think of to stop the escape of freon from the system to no avail. It almost looked like it was snowing at one point in that small part of the stockroom.

We finally realized that we would have to call Delton and Lucretia, on this otherwise quiet Sunday afternoon, to tell them what had happened and ask for assistance. Lucretia entered the store with all the grace and patience of a wounded lion. Delton walked in with a sad disappointed graciousness that was somehow even worse. I explained what had happened and took responsibility for the disaster. Lucretia wanted me fired on the spot. She probably also wanted to carry out some type of drastic public chastisement involving wooden stocks and rotten tomatoes. Delton did a great job of restraining her before she could get her hands on me. I remember standing almost at attention near the store produce display section as Delton quietly told her that he would not fire me. She periodically glanced at me with sidelong lightning bolts emanating from her furious expression as he told her he couldn't afford to fire me until I had a chance to work off the wasted freon. She finally shrugged and stormed out. Delton gave me a stern lecture and I remained on the payroll. It took me several weeks to pay for the damages I had caused in this fiasco. Delton never mentioned it again.

Delton asked me why I had chosen to enlist when he learned that I was about to graduate from high school and enter the army. I told him that I wanted to go to college, but I couldn't afford it and I knew the GI Bill would help me pay for school. He said that he was willing to bet that I would never get any college while I was in the military. I replied, "OK, I'll bet you one hundred dollars that I do get some college while I'm in the army." He reached over, shook my hand, and said, "It's a bet."

I was at home on Christmas leave about two years later and I went by the store to say hello to everyone. Delton greeted me very warmly and then asked if I had been able to get into any college classes yet. I had taken a night class that year, but I had forgotten about our bet. I thought for a moment and said, "Yes. As a matter of fact I took a management class that was offered by the post education center." Delton calmly reached in his pocket and withdrew his wallet. He smiled as he pulled out a crisp one hundred dollar bill and handed it to me saying, "Merry Christmas then!" He didn't have to do this. Simply put, he was a man of his word like my dad. The character and grace shown to me by Delton Wade was a gift from God that has had a lasting effect on me even in some of my worst moments. I know God was using him even then to try and get my attention.

Political turmoil and other factors in the Persian Gulf in the winter of 1973/1974 created a drastic gasoline shortage in the United States. Most of the vehicles that dad had for sale on his lot at the time this crisis started were larger cars. They had been very popular when the average price for a gallon of gas was less than fifty cents. With the new gas crisis, there were times when no gas was available. When it was available, there were huge lines at service stations where people had to wait to purchase fuel. Larger cars were now not only unpopular; you could hardly give them away. All of the smaller vehicles on dad's lot sold very quickly. He was stuck with everything else. The vehicle inventory on the lot was financed through the bank. My parents had used their home as additional collateral for the business financing. Within months they had lost everything. Our family was suddenly bankrupt.

Tough events like this are barely noticed by the local community in a larger city. In small town Bolivar, Missouri, everyone knew what was going on with everyone else. Many of the kids at school were cruel about it. Their attitudes undoubtedly reflected the thoughts and conversations of their parents. We were suddenly forced to move from our new home to the small rental property that my parents now struggled to afford. It was a dramatic step in social class structure from upper middle to where we ended up that year. I guess I didn't notice it as much personally because I was gainfully employed and I owned my own car. My real friends at school and work didn't care about our family's financial difficulties. However, it was quite clear that much of the local business community and many of the people in town were not as readily accommodating.

We were not the only people having trouble that year. Richard Nixon resigned as the 37th president of the United States on August 8, 1974. He was succeeded in the presidency by Gerald Ford. President Nixon had been slowly withdrawing troops from Vietnam for the past several years as he talked about "Vietnamization" in which the South Vietnamese government was made to take over responsibility for their own defense against the communist North Vietnamese and insurgent Viet Cong forces. President Nixon had promised to bring "peace with honor." He barely avoided impeachment by resigning from office following the infamous Watergate Hotel burglary and subsequent cover-up. President Ford basically continued with President Nixon's policies in regard to economics and foreign affairs. I began to worry about what I would do and how I would make a living after I finished school.

My siblings and I, with the exception of our oldest brother, were involved in the youth group at church all through this time. We participated in the activities, went to Sunday school, and listened to the sermons at church. We went to church camp in the summer. We were part of the group, but I didn't really understand what it meant to belong to Jesus. I still went forward at church often when altar calls were given. This was in response to the conviction I felt regarding my lifestyle. I didn't want to go to hell. I was looking for "fire insurance."

I was in a very serious relationship during my senior year in high school with a young lady who had graduated from school the year before. She belonged to a family that was actively involved in the Baptist Church. She intended to go to college at Baylor University in Waco, Texas. She expected me to go there too as soon as I graduated from high school. Conversations about marriage and family obligations began to occur. I had other ideas. I had maintained my desire to join the army since I was in the sixth grade. I considered the cost of college and the certain realization that my grades were horrible. There was no way that my parents would be able to help me financially.

I began talking with the local army recruiter as the middle of the school year arrived. My parents agreed to sign the papers in the middle of February 1975 allowing me to enlist in what the army called a delayed entry program. I wouldn't have to report for active duty until after I had graduated from high school. I chose a four year enlistment as an infantryman with assignment to the 82nd Airborne Division conditional upon successful completion of basic training, infantry school, and jump school. The rest of that school year was more or less uneventful. I turned eighteen right before the end of the school year. I was on a Grey Hound bus two weeks after my high school graduation enroute to the military induction station at Kansas City, Missouri. Life was about to change for me in ways that I didn't have the capacity to understand.

Chapter 4

Soldier Novitiate

*"For the wages of sin is death, but the free gift of God is
eternal life in Christ Jesus our Lord."*
(Romans 6:23)

My time in US Army basic training and infantry school was spent at Ft. Polk, Louisiana. Infantry training had been conducted at Ft. Polk for several years because the climate was very similar to that of Southeast Asia. Saigon, South Vietnam fell to the communists on April 30, 1975 ten days before my 18th birthday and a little over a month before I arrived at Ft. Polk. The Mayaguez incident, in which several US Marines and US Navy personnel were killed trying to free the crew of the merchant ship Mayaguez from Khmer Rouge terrorists on the coast of Cambodia, took place on or about May 15. The US had withdrawn from the war in Vietnam, but there was a general sense that it wasn't really over and that we might be drawn back in somehow.

The Louisiana summer of 1975 was very hot and incredibly humid. It seemed to rain every afternoon just long enough to get everything miserably wet before the sun came back out and turned all of the extra water into steam. The difference between southern Louisiana and anywhere else I had lived was striking. Wild boars roamed the countryside, and alligators swam freely in the waterways and ponds. Snakes and scorpions were prolific, and the mosquitoes were so numerous and large that they seemed like a lethal threat.

I arrived at the training brigade reception station along with a great many other new recruits on June 4, 1975. The personal welcome we received from the drill sergeants at the reception station was shocking, but we hadn't seen anything yet. These noncommissioned officers were only there to receive us and herd us through the inprocessing ordeal of our first week in the army. We would meet our real drill sergeants in another week. I have to admit now that I was scared and had begun to believe that my decision to join the army may have been a mistake. I had to decide that there was no way I was going to quit if all of these other men could do it. This wasn't the last time that my bull-headed stubbornness would serve me well over the next several years.

We were taught the most basic rudiments of who to salute and how to walk and talk during that first week. We were given a merciless series of shots, had our heads shaved, and got issued a great deal of military clothing and personal equipment. The day we got our first military haircuts, we were herded onto a large set of bleachers next to a long narrow building. The building extended out next to and in front of the bleachers on one side. The bleachers continued on the other side of the building. We didn't find that out until after we went through the barber shop. There was a huge crowd of young men with all kinds of long hair in the bleachers on the one side of the building. Everyone in those bleachers seemed to sense the need to comb or pick their hair one last time. It was sad really.

A line was formed from the bleachers to the door of the barber shop. A drill sergeant was standing just outside the door screaming at all the "hippies" in the line waiting to go in. The shop contained three barber chairs in a row with a sea of cut hair covering the floor. The barbers were scalping the recruits as quickly as they could. We were shouted at if we didn't climb in to the first available chair. I think the barber sardonically asked me, "How do you want it?" When I didn't reply, he ran the clippers right over the top of my head from back to front and continued the motion for a few seconds until I was almost completely bald. They yelled at us to get out of the chair and leave the shop to let someone else get "groomed" as soon as we were shorn. I found myself confronted by another giant set of bleachers when I went out the opposite door. These were occupied by hundreds of young men who were all absently massaging their now empty scalps with looks of bemused wonder on their faces. We hadn't been issued any type of uniforms at that point, but we were all beginning to look alike.

We were processed into the system by the end of the week. We were then loaded into what the army called "cattle trucks", and sent to our new training units. These cattle trucks were semi tractor-trailer rigs. The trailers had been designed to carry large numbers of soldiers.

We were carrying all of our newly issued clothing and equipment in duffle bags along with our personal civilian clothing and possessions. The drill sergeants at the reception station ruthlessly packed people into these trailers. We were all standing and trying to keep from crushing each other as the trucks rumbled and rattled across Ft. Polk to our new company areas.

The trucks lurched to a stop when we arrived at the other end. The doors flew open, and we heard almost unintelligible yelling and cursing from our new drill sergeants demanding that we get off their truck and start doing pushups. The drill sergeants were literally grabbing people that seemed to be moving slowly and yanking them off the truck. I was instantly thrust into a bedlam of confusion, cursing, fear, and weird humor. I believe I heard a seemingly furious drill sergeant ask a frightened private "trainee" in a choking roar; "did your parents have any children that lived?" They were always saying stuff like that. Most of these drill sergeants took great pride in turning profanity into an art form. You kind of got used to it after a while. This was never comfortable even if you came to expect it, especially if it was directed at you personally. It was not meant to be.

We learned that we were not yet in the army on this first day in our new training company; we were just "modeling the clothing". We were informed that we would not be considered soldiers until we graduated from basic training a distant nine weeks in the future. We learned that we were no longer lofty civilians because we had lost our minds and agreed to enslave ourselves to the US Government for the length of our individual enlistment contracts. We were told that we were now some type of subhuman creatures known to the underworld and higher life forms as "trainees".

I found myself living in a two story wooden barracks that had been built during WWII. My new training platoon occupied the entire building. Both floors were equipped with rows of double deck bunks down each side from one end to the other. Two vertical wall lockers stood against the wall at the end of each set of bunks. There was an exterior window between each set of bunks and wall lockers. One wooden footlocker sat on the floor under the window, and one wooden footlocker sat on the floor in front of the bunks. These front foot lockers were lined up perfectly with a stripe that had been painted on the floor running the length of the room from front to back. There was an identical arrangement on the other side of the room or "bay". The center floor area between the two stripes was open. We were forbidden to be in this area for any reason other than cleaning and polishing the floor. The only people authorized to walk on this part of the floor were the drill sergeants and any officers or other dignitaries that might find some reason for visiting our lowly abode. This center floor was kept waxed and polished to the point where you could actually see the reflection of the ceiling in the surface. We came to understand that, as far as our drill sergeants were concerned, our character and value as potential humans depended largely on the quality of the shine on that floor.

An open latrine was located at one end of the barracks on the bottom floor. The latrine had a row of toilets along one wall, and a row of sinks and mirrors along the adjacent wall. A washing machine and huge electric clothes dryer sat along the wall opposite the row of toilets. The open showers were entered through a doorway at the back of the latrine. It took a little getting used to the fact that there was absolutely no privacy in this environment.

We were taught the fundamentals of military courtesy and discipline during the first couple weeks of basic training. We learned to recognize the various rank insignia. We learned how to stand at attention, stand at parade rest, and stand at ease. We learned how to march, how to talk, and how to salute. We learned to properly make our bunks, care for our equipment, care for our uniforms, and to spit shine our boots. It took a while, but we gradually learned that the army had its own language, its own justice system, its own culture, and its own rules of social etiquette. We made friends very quickly in that strange new world. We were all in the same mess together and we were expected to begin working together to get through this ordeal. Truth was valued and justice was swift. Almost everything was shared in one way or another. If one of us was in trouble, we were all in trouble.

Some of the best friends I ever had to that point in my life were members of my basic training platoon. We were almost all new to the army and did not yet own any different qualifications. However, most of us had been predestined to certain army divisions or other units. The divisions we would eventually be assigned to had their own distinctive shoulder patches. These patches were sewn onto the left sleeve shoulder of our uniform shirts. We could tell what unit each trainee would eventually end up in if they made it all the way through the qualification and training process as we became accustomed to the different patches.

We also came to recognize that anyone with a unit patch on their right shoulder was a combat veteran. Infantry combat veterans also wore a distinctive emblem attached to their uniforms just above their left breast pockets. This was a long horizontal rectangle enclosing a picture of a flintlock rifle. The rectangle was surrounded by a wreath. We quickly learned from our drill sergeants that this emblem was a Combat Infantry Badge. Most of our drill sergeants had this sacred badge on their shirts along with the shoulder patches of storied infantry divisions on their right shoulders. When we really came to realize what this meant, it made us understand that the wearer of these uniform devices could be trusted as having "been there". We had some younger drill sergeants that were not combat veterans. It was not uncommon for them to have what was called an Expert Infantry Badge on their uniform indicating that they had passed one of the most difficult qualification testing processes in the US military. These noncommissioned officers also demanded and deserved our respect.

Every minute of our day to day existence in basic training was pre-planned and regimented to accomplish the most training possible. The first night in this strange new world, I fell asleep in my bunk with a feeling of loneliness and homesickness that made me absolutely miserable. This wouldn't be the last time I questioned what I had gotten myself into.

We were jarred awake by the shouting of our drill sergeant at about 4:30AM. He was beating on a trash can lid as he stomped up and down in the forbidden center aisle of our barracks bay. This happened almost every morning after that in almost the same way. We rolled out of our bunks and quickly got squared away to start the day. We swiftly learned that personal hygiene was a mandatory requirement in the army. When one of the young men in our barracks displayed an unwillingness to use the community shower, our drill sergeant had us introduce him to what was known as a "GI shower". He was group tackled, dragged to the showers, stripped to his shorts, and washed in cold water with abrasive sink cleanser and stiff brushes. This event reminded me of the "gauntlet" I had seen my brother run through when we were boy scouts. It was effective though, just like the gauntlet, and I never saw this particular trainee avoid the showers again.

We were not allowed to walk anywhere in our company area. We ran everywhere unless we were being marched as a squad, platoon, or company. Every infraction of any rule, either real or imaginary, was punished immediately with a requirement to do pushups. These pushup punishments were usually meted out in groups of ten or twenty repetitions at a time. It wasn't unheard of for more serious failures to require fifty pushups.

The trainees at this stage of their development were in differing physical conditions. Most, like me, were not in bad shape but still had a lot of room for improvement. Some of the young men were slightly overweight. We quickly learned that, in the army, there is no such thing as "slightly overweight". All trainees recognized as belonging to this "mythical" category of subhuman, were mercilessly labeled as "fat boys". They received almost unending torment through extra physical exercise and food deprivation. Any civilian would probably have been appalled at this seemingly inhumane treatment.

However, anyone who was still considered a civilian was not allowed to see what was going on. Besides, the overweight trainees were not considered to deserve humane treatment. They had somehow made it through the pre-screening process to arrogantly show up at basic training with all of their excess weight. In the eyes of the military of the mid 1970s, they were only trainees, and trainees were not quite human anyway.

We began learning about our M16 rifles, gas masks, and other fundamental tools of modern combat as basic training progressed past the third week. We learned to fire and clean our weapons. We were taught how to survive in nuclear, biological, and chemical environments. We learned the code of conduct, and the fundamental aspects of the Uniform Code of Military Justice. We were taught to road march and to establish administrative bivouac sites using pup tents made of shelter halves.

The food was adequate, but we usually had very little time to eat meals. We waited before each meal at parade rest in very long lines that moved slowly forward to the mess hall entrance. Drill sergeants roamed up and down the line looking for any reason to harass the trainees. Short periods of parade rest were punctuated with minutes of agony doing pushups, then a quick lurch to the position of attention, a step forward in the line, and a rigid return to parade rest. We were quickly given the food on our trays when we finally made it through the chow line. We hurried to any open chair at tables in the center of the mess hall and ate as fast as we could while being watched by drill sergeants who roamed the room looking for anything out of place. Each trainee was given about five to ten minutes to eat. We gulped the meals down quickly, dumped the tray, and turned in to the kitchen police. Exiting the doorway on the other side of the mess hall, we ran directly to the barracks to wait for whatever was coming next.

There were representatives from virtually every race and ethnic group in my training unit. There were several men who refused to get along at first. We all eventually realized that there was really only one color represented in our barracks and that was olive drab (OD) green. Everything was OD green. You couldn't escape it. Other colors seemed strange and out of place after a while which made them all the more appealing. We learned more about each other and found that we really had more similarities than differences. Chapel services were available every Sunday, but most of the people in our barracks, including me, chose not to attend. The chaplains seemed nice enough and showed they genuinely cared about the trainees in the command. Church just didn't seem to be a part of the perverse nightmare we all found ourselves in at the time.

I was terribly homesick. I found any opportunity I could to call or write home. Letters from home were incredibly valuable. Mail call was a time of great promise and elation if a letter was received. It was a time of crushing sadness when my name wasn't called as the mail clerk handed out envelopes or packages. I called home collect so often that my dad asked me to stop because they couldn't afford the higher phone bill. I felt bad about it and tried to cut down on the calls. I knew my parents were still struggling financially. I didn't want to make things any worse just because I was lonely. Being lonely among that many other people, who were quickly turning into friends, was a strange experience. On the other hand, I felt like I was finally getting out on my own and becoming an adult with adult freedoms and responsibilities. I missed my family terribly and longed for the happier carefree days of childhood and adolescence.

We spent a great deal of time marching. These marches varied from training in drill and ceremonies, to the long road marches required to reach the training ranges. Every outdoor training station was called a range whether it involved firing weapons, throwing hand grenades, digging fighting positions, applying camouflage, or going through the gas chamber. These training ranges were usually several miles away from the garrison area where our barracks were located.

The drill sergeants would pack us onto the hated "cattle trucks" during the early weeks of basic training. We would be trucked to the ranges and deposited for training. This arrangement didn't last long though. We soon found that we had to walk everywhere we went as a unit, unless the army decided that walking would take too long. As we began to put some real miles on our new combat boots, we often longed for the comfort and rest provided in those cattle trucks.

The drill sergeants called cadence to keep us in step wherever we marched until we were out in the countryside. They would then put us in two long columns on either side of the road and order us to march at "route step". This was usually stretched into what they called a "speed march". The fastest walking drill sergeant would step out into the middle of the road and start walking with long strides as fast as he could. All we had to do was keep up. We were in grave peril if we fell back or fell out. The speed march would continue for what seemed like mile after mile until we didn't think we could go any further. Arriving at the training location or the barracks always brought tremendous relief.

We grew calluses on our calluses just like my experience years earlier when I was chopping fence posts with a dull ax. We developed muscle groups that most of us didn't know existed before. We usually marched or ran as a platoon or company while in the garrison area. The drill sergeants added colorful "Jody" songs to the cadence to keep us in step. After they called a phrase of the song, we were required to repeat it as our left feet struck the ground. Some of these songs were disgusting and some of them were bizarre, but they were all extraordinarily funny. We couldn't help laugh at the perverse humor these drill sergeants were able to come up with even as miserable as we were most of the time. The problem was that punishment was swift if they caught you laughing. It brought a whole new meaning to the old phrase, "It only hurts when I laugh".

I began having severe pain in my right ear about half way through this stage of training. It steadily grew worse over a couple of days. I finally had to go on sick call so that I could visit the infirmary. This was not something that most of us would do willingly. Any visit to sick call could result in time lost from training. That time lost could end up causing the trainee to be "recycled" into another training unit at an earlier place in the training process. This would cause permanent separation from our friends, and would make the misery of basic training go on that much longer.

I did go on sick call this particular day because I just couldn't stand the sharp pain I had in my ear. I really needed to get it taken care of. Upon arrival at the infirmary, I had to wait in a very long line to finally see a medic. The medic looked at me and pushed me on through the process to the point where I found myself being examined by an actual army doctor. The doctor was a female captain. She looked in my ear with her otoscope and became very angry with me. I didn't know what was going on, but I knew better than to react to an officer with disrespect. I asked her what was wrong. She told me that I had a punctured eardrum. She then went on to berate me for "deliberately" puncturing my eardrum just so that I could get out of training. I told her that I had no idea how my eardrum had been punctured, but I sure hadn't damaged it intentionally. I found myself almost begging her to be returned to training. She finally relented and gave me some medicine for the ear and some medicine for the pain. I made it back to the unit and only lost that one day of training. The pain continued for the next week or two, but there was no way I was going to complain about it and get recycled. My best theory was that this injury must have been caused by the hard rubber ear plugs we wore on the rifle and machine gun ranges.

We eventually came to the end of basic training after nine long weeks. The day we graduated, families came to the post to watch the ceremonies. My family couldn't be there. The distance was too great and travel was too expensive. It was nice to see all of the civilians. We really felt like we had accomplished something as we marched in review at our graduation parade. The drill sergeants were a little more civil to us because we were now no longer subhuman trainees. We were still just unskilled private soldiers, and that status was only marginally higher on the military food chain.

We returned to our barracks after the celebration. We were then told what Advanced Individual Training (AIT) units we would be going to. Some of the new soldiers in my unit were being sent to different military installations for this advanced training. Most of us would be loaded back onto cattle trucks to be shipped over to the other side of Ft. Polk for infantry school. I found to my dismay, that I would be separated from the great friends I had made in basic training.

We were soon riding in the cattle trucks with all of our personal and military belongings. The trucks ground to a stop a short while after departure. We found ourselves again being pulled, pushed, and dragged off the trucks by yelling drill sergeants. I soon found that this group of sergeants was even meaner than those we had endured through basic training. These were infantry trainers. The education was about to get very serious and they wanted us to know it. The pushups were unceasing and the running was without mercy for the next couple of hours. We had gone through our graduation from basic training in class B Khaki uniforms. We were still in these same uniforms when we arrived at our new company for infantry school. My uniform was soon soaking wet with sweat in the hot humid Louisiana summer.

We all expected to be released for the weekend following our basic training graduation with what we believed was a well deserved four day pass. My friend Max from New Orleans had invited me to spend the weekend at his parent's home with his family. Max had been assigned to a different company for infantry school. His unit was quickly settled in and released on the coveted pass. Max was standing on the sidewalk at the edge of my company area a short while later trying to get my attention to find out if I would be able to travel home with him. He and some of his other friends had managed to rent a taxi to drive them all the way to New Orleans.

The drill sergeants in my company seemed to take great pleasure letting us know that we would not be given passes to leave if they had any say in the matter. I finally got word to Max to go on without me. I would try to catch up with him if I managed to escape for the weekend. After a couple hours of harassment, our new drill sergeants told us they would let us leave after all if we could pass inspection within thirty minutes. I was frantic to get out of there, but all of my clothing was still stuffed in my duffle bag. The only "good" uniform I had was the one I was wearing and it was soaked with perspiration. I didn't care at that point. I knew they wouldn't let me leave unless I could somehow at least dry the uniform out.

I hurried to the barracks and threw the soaked khaki uniform in the clothes dryer. It dried quickly, but now it smelled horrible. Determined to escape no matter what the cost, I put the same uniform back on and checked to make sure that my brass was somewhat presentable and my shoes were shined. I then ran to the orderly room and reported for inspection. The drill sergeant pretended not to notice the smell and presented me with a pass. There was no time to get cleaned up any better. I hurried to the airport on post. I purchased a ticket on the small prop plane that would travel to New Orleans that afternoon and arrived at the New Orleans airport while it was still daylight. I noticed that I got a lot of strange looks from people on the plane and in the airport, but I didn't care, I was free for a few days. I called Max's house when I landed and spoke with his mom. She told me that Max had not yet arrived. She and his little sister would drive to the airport to pick me up.

Max's mom tried not to react to my rather pungent odor when I got in the car. His little sister tried too, but she was young and not as successful. Max's mom asked me several questions in a subtle effort to figure out why I smelled like a dead goat without embarrassing me as we neared his home. She suggested that I would probably be a lot more comfortable in civilian clothes and offered to lend me some of Max's stuff when we arrived at the house. She then graciously offered to do my laundry. I thanked her profusely and tried to put on some of Max's clothing after taking a luxurious shower. The problem was that Max was about a half foot shorter than I was. His pants ended up looking like knickers on me. I actually wore them until I had clean clothes of my own to wear.

I had been at Max's house for several hours when he called home from a pay phone. His cab ride in a car stuffed with several GIs wasn't as pleasant as my trip by air had been apparently. When he did finally make it home, we spent a great weekend in New Orleans. It was over way too soon, and we were back at Ft. Polk.

Infantry school was much more difficult than basic training. The instruction we were given on small weapons was very extensive. Marksmanship was driven into us with almost religious fervor. There was an intense effort to infuse each of us with intimate knowledge of our individual M16 rifles. We were given detailed training in the use and maintenance of crew served weapons, grenades, light anti tank weapons, mines, and explosives. We spent many days on rifle, machine gun, and grenade ranges. We attended what was called "fire and smoke" school where we learned how to use all kinds of explosives. We were also taught to improvise and use what we could find to make our own explosive devices and booby traps.

Small unit tactical training was relentless. We were taught to function as members of a fire team and rifle squad. This included everything from patrolling to camouflage and construction and occupation of elaborate defensive positions. We learned to communicate with everything from radios to hand and arm signals. The tactical training was very intense and involved what seemed like weeks of repetitive practice in methods of small unit maneuver and movement to contact. We were drilled on battlefield first aid techniques. We learned to defend ourselves with our hands and feet. We were drilled without humor or compassion on the application and purpose of the bayonet, one of the most primitive weapons still in use by modern armies. We were extensively trained on ways to survive in nuclear, biological, or chemical warfare environments.

The Cold War was still very much a fact of life in 1975. We were expected to be able to identify Soviet, and Warsaw Pact vehicles, aircraft, weapons, and equipment as well as those of our NATO allies. Teamwork wasn't just expected, it was demanded without question. The physical training was much more intense, and I soon realized that I was in the best physical condition I had ever known.

We were paid in cash once per month. My monthly pay at this time was a whopping $210. The pay process involved marching to a nearby gymnasium in close formation. When we arrived at the gymnasium, we couldn't help noticing that it was surrounded by military police personnel armed with pistols and army issue 12 gauge shotguns. Our formation was halted near the entrance and we were told to stand at ease. One at a time, we were called out of the formation and told to go inside and report to the pay officer. I saw an officer sitting at a table in the center of the gymnasium floor surrounded by more armed MPs as I entered the building. The table held a large stack of documents that I learned were pay vouchers along with sizeable stacks of brand new ten and twenty dollar bills. We had been sent to report in alphabetical order. I marched directly to the space in front of the table and stopped at rigid attention. We were closely watched and we had to do this correctly. I saluted and held it while almost shouting that I was reporting for pay. The pay officer looked me up and down quickly and demanded my social security number. I recited it. He then took the first pay voucher from the top of the stack and handed it to me asking if it was mine. I barely had time to see my name before he snatched it back and placed it back on the table. He then picked up a stack of bills and began counting out exactly $210 in crisp automaton fashion. He shoved the small pile of bills in front of me and ordered me to sign a receipt that he had placed next to the money. I signed, and he gave me about two seconds to secure the money in my pocket. I saluted again and asked permission to withdraw. He returned the salute and told me to leave. I hurried out a different door as instructed by one of the drill sergeants. I soon found myself in another formation that was slowly growing as each of my fellow platoon members received their pay. We were marched to the post-exchange and allowed to purchase the things we needed. I should add that we had been given a list of required items. By the time these purchases were made, there wasn't much left of a whole month's pay.

I made a lot of friends in infantry school. Most of the men in my new platoon had been in this same company through basic training. The drill sergeants seemed very harsh to me, but these new comrades told me that they had been even worse during basic training. I couldn't fully comprehend that, so I just let it go. We did get a little more freedom on weekends every once in a while. That only meant we could get away from the company area to roam around post for a while on Sundays to go to chapel, visit the PX, or see a movie after our 9:00AM inspection formation.

One of our two platoon drill sergeants had duty as the company charge of quarters (CQ) one Sunday morning. Having CQ duty on a weekend obviously didn't predispose the drill sergeant to any extra expression of kindness toward us. We were standing at rigid attention waiting for him to inspect our uniforms prior to releasing us for the day. He went into the barracks looking for anything out of the ordinary. He walked up and down the side aisles between the bunks and the outside walls pulling on pad locks. He soon found that I had closed the lock but it hadn't actually latched. He stomped back outside and began yelling at all of us as soon as this discovery was made. My security failure caused everyone in the platoon to do extra pushups. The drill sergeant moved quickly up and down the ranks and then released everyone but me. With a look of intense malevolence, he told me to move my wall locker and foot locker out of the barracks and station them in the center of the parade field located next to our company area. I was to report to him at the company orderly room when that was accomplished. It took some effort to drag the lockers out to the parade field, but I finally got it done.

I discovered that the company mortarmen were training on the edge of the field in what seemed like unending repetitions of crew drills with their mortar tubes and aiming stakes. The drill sergeant gave me a broom stick when I reported to him and told me to go back out and guard my lockers since I was too stupid to use the padlock correctly. He instructed me to do rigid facing movements around and around the lockers in the middle of the field as though I was formally guarding a grave site or something of great value. I was to march at rigid attention with the broomstick held at right shoulder arms for nine paces and halt. I would then move the broomstick to port arms and do a right face movement. Returning the broomstick to right shoulder arms, I would take five paces in that direction and halt. I would come to port arms again and do a right face movement. I would return the broomstick to right shoulder arms and take nine paces again. I would march around and around my lockers this way in the blazing sun in the middle of the parade field until he got tired.

This went on and on for what seemed like forever. The drill sergeant's booming voice would float out across the parade field from the screen door on that side of the orderly room every time I paused too long in one of the facing movements. He would shout some perverse insult each time along with an artistically worded threat that would be carried out if I didn't start moving like I had a purpose. The mortar crews were becoming increasingly angry with my presence because I was somehow messing up their drills. They began shouting all kinds of things at me from the other direction. People began stopping their cars out on the street at the edge of the parade field to watch and laugh at my predicament. I'm not really sure how long this went on, but it finally did end and I was able to drag my belongings back into the barracks. I never again left a padlock undone as far as I can remember.

The training became more and more intense as the weeks in infantry school passed. I saw and did things that I wouldn't have believed or understood less than six months earlier. I watched in awe as one young man simply gave up and quit. This man had been in my basic training platoon and had given every indication that he had all of the ingredients for success. The army decided that they didn't want to keep him any more than he wanted to stay when he decided to quit. He was labeled as a "failure to adapt" to military service and given a general discharge. This would automatically change to an honorable discharge six months after his separation from the service.

I had decided long before this that I had made a terrible mistake by joining the army in the first place. There was no way I was going to quit though. It didn't matter what "they" did to me. I was determined to finish this school and get on with it. I'm convinced that most of the young men in my unit felt the same way I did. We were miserable. We were tired. We were lonely, and we were angry. However, we were not going to let our circumstances beat us. We looked around at our drill sergeants and the other army personnel we came in contact with. I believe most of us thought we could do this since they had been able to do it. The training on specific infantry tasks became more intense while the physical training continued to push us to our limit of endurance and beyond.

We finally came near the end of the school, but the demeaning treatment from our trainers was unchanging. In the final few weeks, we began to prepare for our infantry qualification test. This test was the final hurdle we had to overcome before we could graduate from the school. We were told that it would be very difficult. Our drill sergeants began to push our training toward successful completion of the test. There were a large number of specific infantry skills that had to be mastered in order to pass. The time seemed to pass slowly while we were going through this phase, but the day suddenly arrived.

We found ourselves moving to the training range that day with a mixture of relief and dread. The test itself took all day. I don't remember how I did on each of the test stations, but I somehow passed them all and made it to the afternoon. We were given hot chow that evening and prepared for the final requirement for infantry qualification. This was an all night twenty five mile road march.

We were moved onto the road as the day ended. We were all exhausted when we began this very difficult road march strung out on both sides of the road in long single files. The sun went down and night came with us moving along the road at a steady pace. I experienced something that night that I had noticed before and have endured on other occasions since. It is possible to go almost sound asleep while walking in a large group at night. Strict noise and light discipline was being enforced. We couldn't talk with each other. We weren't close enough to each other to converse anyway. The clanking rhythm of canteens and rifle straps combined with fatigue and the monotonous continual movement seemed to draw us into a kind of hypnotic sleep. One of our officers called a ten minute halt after what seemed like several hours into the march. I was startled to blunder into the man in front of me. The short break allowed some momentary relief, but made the misery more pronounced when we were ordered to move out again.

The march went on the rest of the night. Our unit moved down the road in an almost invisible double line of exhausted soldiers. All of us were drawn along as we mechanically followed the quiet rhythmic clinking equipment of the men in front of us. We almost felt pushed along at the same time by similar noise coming from behind us. It was so dark that we could barely see anything at all for several hours. We were finally able to make out the terrain features and the dark ghostly forms of the men around us as dawn neared. We were entering an area where there were more and more buildings along the roadside. We slowly started to hear the faint sound of band music in the distance.

We soon noticed we had entered a part of Ft. Polk that we were not very familiar with. It was clearly a part of the garrison area of the post. One of the drill sergeants brought us to a halt a few minutes later and quickly formed us into a regular column of four files. We were then moved out at quick-time march cadence and told to straighten our shoulders and pick our chins up. The band music was louder now.

We came slowly around a bend in the road and saw a group of officers and sergeants in an otherwise empty parking lot out ahead of us. The band was standing in a tight formation to the side of the lot. We were marching in step with the music. We realized, in a steadily clearing fog, that the band was there for us. The officers and non-commissioned officers were there for us as well. There may have been civilians in the area also, but I don't remember seeing any.

This was a decidedly "infantry" moment. We were marched into the middle of the parking lot and brought to a relieved halt. We were faced to the left toward the group of officers and told to dress our lines. Standing at exhausted but rigid attention, we were informed that we were now accepted as infantrymen in the United States Army. We were given our new blue shoulder ropes and blue plastic discs to put under our uniform brass. We were given blue neck-cloths to wear under our filthy fatigue uniform shirts. We were welcomed as little brothers into a very special fraternity called the infantry. After this "Turning Blue" ceremony, we were marched to our company area and released for the rest of the day. Our drill sergeants changed after that. Official graduation from infantry school came a few days later and was sort of anti-climactic.

Most of our unit moved on immediately to their permanent duty post destinations. However, a couple of my friends and I were ordered to stay at Ft. Polk so that we could go through a week long training program on the Dragon anti-armor weapon system. We continued to live through that week in the same barracks we had been in through infantry school. It was strange and kind of lonesome staying in that now nearly empty barracks. The three of us received qualification certificates as Dragon gunners when that week was over. We were loaded on a bus headed to Ft. Benning, GA for jump school. The memory of that morning "Turning Blue" ceremony brings a flood of powerful emotion even now. We had finally been fully accepted back into the human race.

Chapter 5

Acrophobic Optimist

*"For by grace you have been saved through faith.
And this is not your own doing; it is the gift of God,
not a result of works, so that no one may boast."*
(Ephesians 2:8, 9)

I arrived at Ft. Benning, Georgia after a very long bus ride with my friends Terry and Wayne. I immediately noticed the three famous 250 foot tall parachute training towers surrounded by a paved running track and a large number of smaller training towers and contraptions. Our new home was a three story cinder block barracks located in a row of buildings at the side of the running track. It was early October, but it was still hot in southern Georgia.

The sergeant that greeted our bus was carrying a clipboard and wearing a maroon (red) beret. We were amazed that we were greeted with something that seemed like friendliness, although my two friends and

I were still privates. We were quickly given our barracks assignment and told to make ourselves at home. We would not be expected to show up for work until the next morning at first formation. We were free to do whatever we wanted. This reception seemed very strange after what we had experienced at Ft. Polk. I discovered that my pay records had been lost in transition to Ft. Benning during the process of signing in to the training unit. I didn't know it at the time, but this would haunt me for almost a year before the army was finally able to stop paying me in temporary "casual-pay loans" and reconstruct my payroll records.

We were told that we would be enduring what the army called a "filler week" when we reported for duty the next morning. The training company we were in didn't yet have enough students to allow it to start the jump school training process. Over the next week, we would be kept busy by doing work details all day every day until the company reached its required size. The chores in these work details involved any kind of mundane manual labor that the person in authority could think up. We picked up trash and cigarette butts all over post and pulled grass and weeds out of sidewalk cracks until our fingers felt like they were coming off. At the same time, we watched other units going through different phases of ground school and tower school in their parachute training. It was a very long week.

I was promised a bonus of two thousand dollars at the time I joined the Army for enlisting in a combat arms occupational specialty for a period of four years. This bonus was given to me in the form of a check at the end of infantry school. I mailed the check home to mom for safe keeping. I now decided to use it to buy a car and asked her send the check back to me. Two thousand dollars was quite a fortune to an eighteen year-old in October of 1975. Late one day, after many hours of filler week details, I was of post and found a 1971 Ford Mach I Mustang. This was a muscle car. It had a 351 cubic inch V8 engine with Cleveland heads. It also had a four speed manual transmission with Hurst Competition Plus linkage. I bought the car and decided to make it into even more of a hot-rod. My friend Terry and I took it to a local garage in Columbus and persuaded the garage owner to let us keep the car there while we worked on it. He also agreed to help us with some of the work for a pretty reasonable price. After that, we spent most of our evenings at the garage working on that car. With the modifications we made, it soon became a monster street-rod that could possibly have been competitive for drag racing if I had been back in the sleepy town of Bolivar, Missouri. I knew my brother Steven would love it.

We were dismayed to learn that the company still hadn't grown enough to start the actual training process at the end of our first jump school "filler week". Another filler week was planned. Our company commander introduced us one morning to a young lieutenant with some very interesting information. The lieutenant told the formation that he had a special opportunity for as many as four soldiers who chose to volunteer. Terry, Wayne, and I knew better, at this point, than to volunteer for anything. The lieutenant kept talking and eventually got around to delivering the rest of his sales pitch. We finally realized what this "opportunity" was about.

All three of us immediately shot our hands in the air and stepped forward when called out of the formation. The lieutenant explained that he was going to be responsible for a special jump school company. This special company would experience a jump school training schedule that had been shortened to allow army reservists and national guard members to complete the school during their two week annual training period. He needed volunteers from our company to finish filling the class. There would be no weekend break and the normal three week school would be compressed into fourteen days. Each day would involve as much training as the army could get into it. This seemed a lot better than the revolting idea of spending another week or two pulling grass out of sidewalk cracks. We soon gathered our gear and reported to the barracks next door.

Jump school started for the three of us on the next day. We found ourselves standing in a very large formation surrounded by old army reservists and national guard members of almost every rank and age. We could not help noticing the peculiar presence of three navy SEALs at the back of the formation. These SEALs had recently graduated from their training in San Diego, and had to get parachute qualified. The navy had sent them to Ft. Benning to go through the army parachute school. The SEALs were in this particular class formation because they also saw an opportunity to get through this training quickly.

The training formation was being held in a large paved lot with steel cables stretched across it from side to side about 18 inches high. There was a cable for each rank of the formation. We were lined up and standing at rigid attention with our shins pressing against the cable in front of us. If I remember correctly, the senior member of the class was a lieutenant colonel. The class also included a large number of majors, captains, lieutenants, and senior sergeants.

Our cadre members in basic training and infantry school had been drill sergeants who wore the infamous round "Smokey the Bear" campaign hats. The cadre members at jump school were all experienced jump master qualified sergeants who wore T-shirts and black baseball caps. They inevitably became known as "black hats". We didn't have long to wait in that first formation for our introduction to the black hats. A sizeable group of them marched up in front of us and stopped.

Their leader approached the colonel who was standing out in front of our formation and saluted crisply. He then let it be known in no uncertain terms that this was the last time any rank would be recognized during this school. He informed all of us, officers and enlisted personnel alike, that we would be treated as equals and expected to perform any and every task given to us without hesitation or question.

The rest of the black hats then descended on us like locusts on a field of wheat. They moved up and down the ranks of students stopping in front of each person. Looking the student up and down, they would either ask some kind of weird question or just make some absurd derogatory remark. When the question couldn't be answered, or the response wasn't just right, they would order the student into what they called the "front leaning rest" position. This position involved "reclining" in a prone "pushup" position with your legs elevated on the steel cable.

There were almost one hundred students standing in this formation when the training day started. My two friends and I were somewhere near the middle of the third or fourth rank. When the black hats finally reached us, they found the three of us standing at rigid attention expecting more of the kind of harassment and purposeful hazing we had endured all the way through infantry school. The black hat in front of me stopped and looked appraisingly at all three of us. He then asked if we had just come through infantry school at Ft. Polk. I shouted, "yes sergeant!" He looked at his companion and smiled knowingly. He then did something shocking to all three of us. He simply walked on to the next reservist beyond my friend further along in the rank. All but six of the people that had been standing in that formation earlier were sweating and groaning as they struggled to do elevated pushups a short while later. The six exceptions were those three navy SEALs, my two friends, and me. The rest of our time in jump school wasn't like this, but the surprising respect shown to us that day by these hard-ened army professionals was not lost on anyone there.

The ground week portion of the US Army parachute school involves a tremendous amount of physical training or "PT". Each day started with a couple of laps around the 2.5 mile airborne track. These runs were done in close formation. Everyone's left foot struck the ground at the same time as cadence was called by a black hat running at the side of our formation. The cadence calls were shouted back by the students in formation as our left feet struck the ground on the next step. The resulting repeated chant was loud and rhythmic. As the run pro-gressed, we soon found ourselves rocking along in this strangely hypnotic rhythm. I now understand that these runs were made much easier to endure in this way.

We were watched closely. The uniform we all wore for this training included T-shirts, fatigue pants, and leather combat boots. We were required to shout out loudly as we ran. Falling out of (or quitting) any of the phys-ical training was inexcusable. We usually ate breakfast after completing our morning run and then re-formed for more physical training. The training was done at different stations, and we always ran from one station to another.

The station we spent the most time in during the first few days of the school was called the "sawdust pit". This was literally a large covered area with a floor that was full of sawdust to a depth of at least a foot. We would march into the pit in formation. The black hat would then spread the formation out so that each student had plenty of room. We would go through a number of exer-cises from that position. These were meted out in rep-etition quantities intended to bring everyone to muscle failure and beyond.

The favorite exercise was, of course, the pushup. There was now a new torture that seemed to be loved by anyone wearing a black baseball cap. This exercise was called the "body twist". You dropped onto your back in the sawdust for this one and held your arms out to your sides. You lifted your legs straight up in the air with your feet and knees together. At the command to begin the exercise, the black hat would call a four count cadence. At the count of one, you twisted your legs over to the left without bending at the knees until your feet were about ten inches from the sawdust. At the count of two, you moved your legs back up to vertical. At the count of three, you moved your legs over to the right. At the count of four, you moved your legs back up to vertical. Everyone in the pit would shout the repetition number. Without missing a beat, the black hat would continue with another four count repetition, and then another, and another, and another until it seemed like your abdomen was going to tear itself apart.

Anyone who failed to continue these exercises, or fell out of a run, was mercilessly tormented with further exercises and red faced mouth frothing verbal abuse. The student soon disappeared from the school if they continued to fail physically. Our physical training was not limited to the running track and the sawdust pit. There were other stations that involved pull-up bars and horizontal ladders. It didn't take a MENSA candidate to understand that the army was intent on determining our upper body and abdominal strength and our overall capacity for physical endurance.

We visited actual technical training stations between physical training sessions in the sawdust pit. These included the swing landing trainer, the lateral drift trainer, and parachute landing fall or "PLF" platforms. We came to know the swing landing trainer as "suspended agony". This device required the student to climb a high platform and strap into a parachute harness with risers that were suspended from the ceiling. On command, we would jump off the platform and hang in the harness as we were drilled through a series of steering and control maneuvers called "slips". We would hang there in the agony created by the ill fitting harness until we showed that we could properly perform the maneuvers. We would then be pushed into a swinging motion and released to do a parachute landing fall on the sawdust below.

We learned everything about the army T-10 parachute and how to use it properly. We were taught the different functions of every part of the parachute system and how they interacted with each other. We learned to properly put on the harness, how to steer the chute in the air, and how to get out of the harness safely on the ground. To this end, we were strapped into parachute harnesses and pulled or blown across a field while we fought to disengage the quick release mechanism on one of the shoulder riser straps. If you didn't get it to release, you continued to get dragged.

We were taught all of the various jump commands and safety procedures. This part of the training occurred while we were still on the ground. It was also done while we were physically exhausted. At about mid-day, we would run from the training area to the mess hall and have a quick lunch. We then formed back up and ran back to the training area for more physical training and more technical instruction. As we completed each of these days, we usually finished with another lap around the airborne track.

Ground week was intended to be completed over the period of a week. We were doing the school on the accelerated "reservist schedule". The same amount of training had to be completed. We just had to do it in fourteen days rather than twenty one. This meant that the first five days were used for ground week, the next six days were reserved for tower week, and the final three days would be jump week if we made it that far.

Each student had to demonstrate complete competence with all of the parachute technical components in order to proceed from ground week to tower week. We had to fully understand all of the emergency procedures and jump commands. We had to show that we could do parachute landing falls properly. We also had to pass a physical training test which included a required number of regular army pull-ups on a horizontal bar. It was surprising to see how many people couldn't do these pull-ups even though they were able to do everything else. Those who failed in any of the required tasks didn't move on through the training.

Tower week was the longest part of the school. Training in this segment was, of course, done using various towers as the name implies. We still started our mornings with long physical training runs on the airborne track, but the long sessions in the sawdust pits were left behind after ground week.

The primary training devices during this phase of the school were the 34 foot jump towers and the 250 foot free release towers. The 34 foot jump tower consisted of a mock-up airplane fuselage door section positioned on stilts so that the floor of the fuselage was 34 feet in the air. There were stairs leading up to the fuselage from the ground below. One aircraft door was positioned on each side of the fuselage, and a heavy steel cable ran horizontally on each side of the fuselage above the doors to an earthen berm about fifty yards away. Several parachute harnesses were attached to each of these steel cables with pulley wheels that allowed the riser harnesses to "ride" the top of the cable.

We were introduced to training on this tower with the usual screaming punctuated by pushups. Use of this tower involved running up the stairs to the fuselage, then very quickly putting on one of the attached harnesses. We would join the "stick" of other jumpers that had reached the fuselage before us. A black hat was stationed inside the aircraft door in what would normally be the jumpmaster position. Another black hat was seated on what looked like a very tall lifeguard chair that was located outside facing the door about fifteen yards away.

We shuffled toward the door with the exit of each successive jumper. We had to turn into the door and pause when we reached it. We were required to assume what the black hats' described as a perfect door position with our hands on the outside of the doorway, our knees slightly bent, and our eyes looking straight out at the horizon. At the command of "go" we were supposed to jump up six inches and out thirty six inches. As we exited the door, we moved our hands immediately to cover the sides of the reserve parachute fastened to the front of the harness at waist level with our right hands protecting the rip cord handle. We had to form our bodies into a rough "L" shape with our chins on our chests, our knees locked, and our feet out in front of us.

The riser straps on the harnesses used for the 34 foot tower were about fifteen feet long. We fell until we reached the end of the straps when we jumped out the door, and learned abruptly whether or not we had put the harness on correctly. Gravity asserted itself at that point, and we rode down the steel cable via the pulley system to the dirt berm where we were caught by a couple of fellow students. We ran to the base of the lifeguard chair for critique after quickly getting disconnected from the cable. The critique usually included a memory enhancement method involving pushups.

All this repetitive instruction was designed to force us into the correct body position when jumping. This was intended to keep our parachute risers and suspension lines from getting twisted by the slip stream spinning our bodies when we exited from a high performance aircraft. The black hats demanded perfection in each door exit. They watched everything we did very closely. If we did it right, we did it again. If we didn't do it right, we still did it again after getting screamed at and doing more pushups.

We did this over, and over, and over again for days. In order to qualify on this tower, each student had to do five perfect door exits as judged by the black hats. To make this more difficult, the five perfect exits had to be done sequentially. If we did three perfect exits, then messed up on the fourth attempt, we had to start all over again. This was much more difficult than it seems now. The black hats meant it when they described a performance standard as "perfect". We could not proceed to the next part of the training without achieving this standard. People that couldn't achieve it eventually disappeared from the program.

I realized I was desperately afraid of heights during tower week. This seems funny now, but at the time, I wasn't laughing. We proceeded to train on grounded steel frame aircraft fuselage mock-ups after days of enduring the 34 foot jump tower and finally attaining the requisite five "perfect" door exits. Here, we relearned all of the jump commands by heart through exhaustive repetition.

We then progressed to the 250 foot free release towers. There are three of these towers at Ft. Benning. As far as I know, they're still there. They were originally designed for the World's Fair sometime in the 1920s. Someone from army procurement saw them at the fair and Uncle Sam bought them. They were moved to Ft. Benning right before the US entered WWII and they have been there ever since.

These towers were very sturdy steel frame contraptions. They each had four arms that stuck out horizontally. From these arms, a steel cable was suspended that could be raised and lowered all the way from the ground to just under the end of the arm. A control room was located inside each tower base. A large round hoop was suspended from chains that kept the hoop hanging horizontally like a giant chandelier frame at the working end of the steel cable. Hundreds of mechanical clips were attached to the sides of these hoops, and a single larger clip was attached to the cable itself at the apex of the whole assembly.

Use of this training device involved getting into a parachute harness that was part of an old T6 parachute. The parachute was open. The student victim was clipped into the hoop by about twenty fellow students working under the close supervision of a black hat. The apex clip held the top of the parachute canopy. The clips on the side of the hoop held the edges of the canopy open. A 50 foot safety strap was clipped to one of the D-rings on the front of the parachute harness, then run over the side of the hoop and back to the harness where it was again clipped to the D-ring. The black hat then shouted instructions to the tower operator in the control room with a hand held megaphone, and the entire assembly was drawn upward to the top of the tower with the student dangling below the open parachute.

That was when I realized that I was desperately afraid of heights. Two hundred fifty feet may not seem like it's very high. It doesn't look high when you are standing on the ground looking up at it. I was up there. It's a lot higher than you think. I trained on this monstrosity. I again questioned the wisdom of my decision to become a paratrooper as I reached the top of the tower and the ascension stopped with a mechanical lurch.

I could barely hear the black hat on the ground as he yelled at me through the megaphone. A few seconds passed. I understood that he wanted me to undo my safety strap. I thought about that for a moment, but finally realized that there was no honorable way around it. I slowly undid the clips holding the strap to my harness D-ring. I pulled it through the hoop and dropped it to the ground. It seemed to take a long time to fall to the dirt below. The people on the ground standing around looking up at me seemed very tiny.

This was sort of like hanging from an arm protruding from the top of a twenty five story building. I suddenly heard a tiny voice of command from the black hat with the megaphone. The cable lurched upward about five feet and all of the clips sprang open to release the parachute canopy. I was free from the tower and moving toward the ground. It wasn't as bad as I thought it would be after the first heart stopping moment. In fact, I was kind of enjoying it until I again realized that the black hat was yelling at me with his megaphone. He was telling me to maneuver with riser slips and prepare for impact with the ground. I was still required to do this correctly, and I would soon learn that there was a reason for the heavily practiced parachute landing fall.

A standard military parachute functioning correctly slows the parachutist to an impact speed of about 24 feet per second on a still day. Any surface wind speed is added to the vertical impact speed. In other words, even on a calm day, you hit the ground at about the same speed you would experience if you jumped off the roof of a single story house. Legs, feet, and other append-ages are often broken when this is done incorrectly. That's why we spent so much time training on how to do it right. I hit the ground hard. I really don't remember what happened next because I was so happy to be on the ground in the first place. I probably did a lot of pushups for landing like a slab of beef. I really don't remember a lot about the rest of tower week, but I made it through somehow.

Jump week was the shortest segment of this school. For reasons that might seem obvious, it was also the most traumatic. On the first day of this segment, we were marched to the nearby airfield and held in for-mation until we were moved into a large hangar on the edge of the field. This hangar doubled as a storage facility and large classroom. Seated in the classroom area, we received some lectures and listened with stoic endur-ance as loud speakers blasted traditional songs with lyrics that were intended to add fear to this already ter-rifying process.

I had learned to control my fear, but I still wasn't enjoying this. I prayed that God would forgive my sins and protect me through this ordeal. I wasn't actually repenting. I didn't really know what the word repent meant. I was just looking for "fire insurance". I had finally come to the brilliant conclusion that I was actually mortal. I remembered all the fire and brimstone descriptions of hell that I had heard when I was in church. I wanted none of it. I knew I was a sinner. I knew I deserved punishment in eternal hell and sensed that the preachers were right. There was nothing I could do to save myself. I had been taught since early childhood that God had sent His only Son Jesus to die in my place so that my sins could be forgiven. I was again stumped by the fact that I couldn't stop sinning, and I didn't know what to do about it.

We were organized into what were called "chalk" numbers. A plane load of jumpers was called a "chalk". The file of jumpers that would exit through the door on one side of the plane was called a "stick". The jumper that would exit the plane first in each stick was called the "door man". We were called out of the classroom area that first morning by chalk number and moved in single file to where we were each issued an expertly packed T-10 main parachute, a reserve parachute, and a canvas kit bag. From there we moved outside to the tarmac and began putting on our parachutes under close supervision in a loose formation. Once this was done, we underwent the required jump master inspection of our gear. We were then reformed and I was in the rear rank of the formation at the right end.

We were given the command to face left and I found myself at the end of the column. I felt momentary relief as I thought I would be at the back of the stick. We were marched out onto the tarmac toward the "tailgate" of a parked C141 jet cargo plane. As the formation marched

straight up the tailgate into the plane, I suddenly realized that being at the end of the column meant that I
would end up at the back of the airplane. I was going to
be the door man for the left aircraft door. My heart was
pounding nearly out of my chest. My knees were weak
as I bent over to sit down on the web seat assembly that
was located right next to the door frame.

The C141 was a four engine jet aircraft. When used
for this purpose, it had two rows of inboard web seats
positioned back to back running the length of the cargo
hold. It also had two rows of outboard web seats that ran
the length of the cargo hold along the aircraft walls. The
plane would hold 70 fully equipped military parachutists in two sticks of 35. Two steel cables ran along the
top of the cargo hold from front to back just above the
area where each stick stood while they were preparing
to exit the plane.

Normal parachute operations on this plane required
one "jump master" per door backed up by another qualified person who acted as the "jump master safety". All
US Army jump masters are highly trained and heavily
experienced professionals. The jump masters working in
the parachute school at Ft. Benning then and now were
and are the best of the best. The C141 air crew included
the pilot, copilot, and two load masters.

Army airborne enlisted personnel in those days were
paid an additional $55 per month "hazardous duty" pay
as long as they made at least one parachute jump every
thirty days. Commissioned officers received $110 in
extra "incentive" pay for the same reason. Our plane that
morning had a group of four extra jumpers. These men
were black hats who needed to make this jump so that

they could continue to receive their hazardous duty pay. These black hat sergeants were wearing black fatigues and black motorcycle helmets instead of the OD green fatigues and steel helmets the rest of us had on. They took seats directly across from me in the inboard row near the door. We were told that they were going to act as "wind dummies" on the first pass.

We quickly sat down and strapped in. The air was thick with an almost tangible sense of fear. The tailgate slowly closed, and the aircraft taxied out to the end of the active runway for take-off. We learned that the plane would be in flight for 45 minutes before we jumped. A river borders Ft. Benning on that side, and the drop zone used by the school was located just across the river in Alabama. I learned later that the reason for the 45 minute flight before our exit was because the pilots needed to be able to record at least one hour of flight time in their pilot logs. I can't remember all of the thoughts that went through my mind during that flight, but I know I probably did a lot of praying as I tried to make a "deal" with God. It wasn't long before we witnessed a spectacle that left me terror stricken and struggling to breathe.

The air force load master was wearing what looked almost like a space suit to me. I suddenly noticed him in this strange costume as he came walking toward the rear of the plane along the top of the rail that separated the inboard rows of seats. When he reached the back of the plane, he jumped down and said something to the jump masters. They all stood up from their seats, and the load master stepped over to the door. He began working with the door controls, and both doors soon came open, sliding up into the roof of the fuselage.

A step plate extended the floor out beyond the doorway a few inches, and wind deflectors were extended out about a foot in front of the leading edge of each door. Even with these deflectors in place, the wind was now whipping madly around in the rear of the airplane. The noise was incredibly loud. I was sitting in a jump seat right next to the leading edge of the left aircraft door. I couldn't help myself. I had to look out. I was able to see the ground below us in clear detail. We were flying at an altitude of only 1250 feet. I could see roads, houses, and small wisps of cloud passing under the plane at very high speed.

The load master positioned himself on the other side of the door from me. The jump master in charge of my door stepped up and into it while the jump master safety stood behind him and held onto his parachute harness from behind. The jump master was wearing a "free fall" style parachute. The jump master safety was attached to the inside of the aircraft with a heavy safety strap and harness. The jump master held on to both sides of the door as he carefully examined the inside and outside of the door frame. He was inspecting the door opening for any deformities or sharp edges. He took a brief moment to lean out and look forward toward our intended drop zone. As he looked out, I was watching his face. The wind distorted the skin on his face as he struggled to see.

The C141 is a heavy airplane. If there is no substantial head wind, it must move at about 200 miles per hour ground speed just to maintain level flight. Someone told me at some point that, when they are delivering paratroopers from this plane, the pilots bring the inboard set of engines to idle to keep the jet exhaust from burning the chutes as the jumpers exit the doors. I wasn't thinking about anything like that at this particular moment.

The jump master heaved himself back when he was finished inspecting the doorway and turned to face the inboard aircraft seats. He then shouted instructions at the "wind dummies" sitting across from me, telling them to "Stand up!" The four black hats stood up and folded their jump seats into the stowed position. This was followed immediately with a shouted instruction to "Hook up!" They each disconnected the clips on the ends of their parachute static lines from the carrying handles on the tops of their reserve parachutes and connected them to the steel anchor line cable above their left shoulders. Taking a "reverse bite" grip on the static lines with their left hands, they each quickly ensured that the line was freely draped over their left shoulders to the main parachute packs on their backs.

The jump master shouted, "Check equipment!" They each checked their own reserve chutes and the harness assembly that they could see in front of them. They then quickly checked the equipment on the back of the jumper nearest them. A few seconds later, the jump master shouted, "Sound off for equipment check!" The jumpers were standing in a single file "stick" facing the jump master in the door area at the back of the plane. The jumper nearest the front of the plane slapped the next man on the back and shouted "OK!" That man in turn slapped the next man on the back and shouted "OK!" That man did the same thing. The door man then held up his right hand and shouted, "All OK!"

The jump master turned and quickly spoke with the load master. There were two signal lights attached to the inside trailing edge of the doorway at the top. One of the lights was red and the other was green. The green light was off and the red light was glowing brightly. The jump master turned back toward the jumpers and shouted, "Three minutes!" A brief interval screamed past. The jump master shouted, "Thirty seconds!" Another few seconds passed. The jump master then quickly stepped once to his right and pointed at the doorway shouting, "Stand in the door!" The door man moved to the spot right in front of me and stopped immediately in front of the leading edge of the doorway facing out at a slight angle.

This was a different door position than the one we had been drilled on so diligently during Tower Week. Our instructors had explained to us that the procedure had to be adjusted when jumping from a jet because the airplane was traveling much faster than a prop driven aircraft. With this plane, you didn't jump up 6 inches and out 36 inches, you just stepped out at an angle and the slip-stream did the rest of the work for you.

The green light blinked on suddenly and the red light went off. The jump master shouted, "Go!" The black hat that had been right in front of me a moment before was suddenly gone! The second one followed a moment later, and then the third, and the fourth. I watched in terrorized fascination as the last man shot down and away from the back of the aircraft. His fifteen foot static line zipped out of the keepers on the back of his chute in a lightning fast second and the cotton tie snapped releasing his deployment bag from the pack tray. In the next second the fifteen foot long suspension lines and the risers freed themselves from the pack tray and fully extended. The parachute canopy whipped out of the deployment bag instantly and the last cotton tie broke freeing the parachute and jumper from the plane. The canopy filled with air and opened round and green as the image became rapidly smaller and then disappeared in the distance.

I watched these things happen from my seat with my heart almost frozen in fear. The four static lines were still streaming out of the doorway with the attached deployment bags whipping in the wind. The load master quickly attached a hook and cable to the set of static line clips and they were pulled back into the plane by the hydraulic static line retriever. When this was done, the load master closed both doors and the plane began a slow bank out of the area. This whole process had happened very quickly. I was relieved when the doors closed, until I realized that this had just been the "first pass" and my turn was next.

Several minutes passed as the aircraft made some sweeping turns to circle the drop zone and set up for another long deliberate approach. A short while later, the load master again opened the doors and stowed them near the roof inside the plane. The jump masters stood up and shouted, "Outboard personnel, stand up!" This time, both doors were in operation almost independently of one another. The jump masters would send each jumper out through their doors at one second intervals in such a way that there was a half second interval between each door. This would keep the jumpers leaving each door from colliding with each other as they reached the area behind the aircraft.

I undid my seat belt, stood woodenly to my feet, and struggled for a few seconds to bend over and stow my web seat. The jump master shouted, "Inboard personnel, stand up!" The men sitting in the inboard rows stood up, stowed their seats, and merged with the men that were already standing. The jump master shouted, "Hook up!" I disconnected my static line clip from my reserve carrying handle and connected it to the anchor line cable. As I established what felt like a death grip on the static line reverse bite, I barely heard the rest of the jump commands.

I was staring straight at the jump master's face. He was shorter than me, and I can still remember the shiny OD green steel helmet he was wearing. He was a master sergeant and his rank insignia was prominently displayed on the front of the helmet in gold paint. I checked the harness and equipment that I could see on the front of my body and felt the slap on my back when the jumper behind me shouted "OK!" I mechanically raised my right hand and shouted, "All OK!"

The jump master turned slightly to listen to the load master and then turned back to shout, "Six minutes!" He moved into the doorway with help from the jump master safety, and did another quick examination of the door opening. The jump master drew himself back from the door again, and looked me right in the eyes as he pointed to the doorway and shouted, "Stand in the door!"

I remember that I was thinking this was just some kind of terrible nightmare. I wasn't really here participating in this insanity. My body automatically moved toward the doorway and my left hand mechanically released the static line as the jump master safety took control of it. The jump master told me to hold onto some conduit that ran along the inside of the leading door edge and coaxed me into the proper angle in relation to the doorway. With his face close to my left ear, he shouted over the terrific noise asking me if I was alright. I shouted as I had been trained to respond to any question from a black hat, "Yes sergeant, airborne!"

I started looking in terrified fascination out the door and down toward the ground passing under the aircraft at high speed. The jump master told me to look up and fix my attention on the horizon. He then told me not to pay attention to the red and green lights in the door frame. I was listening to him and acting like I was in agreement with everything he said, but my brain was telling me something completely different.

There was no way this was going to happen. I was not doing this. It didn't matter what they did to me, I was not going to go through with this very bad plan. Time had slowed down in an almost incredible fashion. The jump master suddenly shouted, "Three minutes!" He then started talking to me again about my body position and where to fix my gaze. He suddenly shouted, "Thirty seconds!"

The jump master then moved very close to my left side and said, "Don't worry about the lights! When I hit you on the leg and say go, just walk right out the door at an angle! Do you understand?" What could I say? I responded with the same shouted, "Yes sergeant, airborne!" He then almost calmly shouted "OK, go!" as he slapped me on the back of my left thigh.

My body simply moved itself to the required body exit position without consulting my brain and stepped out the door. I was staring at the toes of my boots as I fell away from the plane. It was strangely similar to riding down some type of giant slide, except that I had the added sensation of encountering the 200 MPH slip-stream and the incredibly loud engine noise just outside the aircraft.

The jumper was supposed to measure the seconds after exiting the plane when this was done correctly. If the main parachute canopy had not opened within six seconds, it meant that there had been a total malfunction of the main parachute mechanism. The jumper was then supposed to immediately turn his head to the left and pull the rip cord handle on the reserve parachute. When this handle was pulled, the spring loaded reserve parachute would be ejected into the air in front of the jumper's body and immediately open. The reserve parachute would save the jumper's life, if it was opened soon enough, even though this canopy was smaller than the main chute and its location on the harness would force the jumper to land backwards. Once a jumper's body cleared the aircraft and reached what was called "terminal velocity", he was falling at about 100 feet per second. There was very little time to react in this type of emergency. Most military "static line" parachute jumps like this were conducted at an altitude of around twelve hundred feet.

I was supposed to be counting in thousands to measure the amount of elapsed time from exit, but I don't remember doing that. On that first jump, I don't think I would have reacted in time to save my life if my parachute had totally malfunctioned. I would have reached the ground way before anyone else. As mentioned in one of the most popular "Jody songs", the black hats would have probably insisted that my remains be buried in the "front leaning rest" position. Again, God was looking out for me and protecting me even though I had cynically been praying for "fire insurance". His awesome grace is often displayed most prominently like this in our times of greatest weakness.

The parachute assembly did function properly this time. I soon felt the harness tighten as the canopy opened and yanked my body into the feet down position. My risers were twisted because my body had spun in the exit blast. My head was being held down by the risers. I reached up to pull the risers apart so that I could look up and see a beautiful OD green parachute canopy.

The sound of the plane flying away reminded me oddly of the noise that my mom's old torpedo vacuum cleaner used to make. I looked in that direction and saw the other jumpers exiting both sides of the aircraft in half second intervals. They looked like green eggs being laid by some giant metal monster that grew quickly smaller and quieter as it flew into the distance. The sky was bright blue and the sun was shining warmly. I felt a euphoria that I can't quite find words to describe.

We soon began to hear the faint sound of black hats on the ground yelling up at us again through megaphones. A small creek runs through this particular drop zone lengthwise as I recall. The black hats were telling me and the other jumpers in the air to pull riser slips to avoid landing in the creek. I was feeling great at this point, and it didn't seem like I was descending at all. I began pulling down on the risers on one side to let more air spill out of the other side of the canopy and "push" me in the direction I wanted to slip. Looking between my toes, I could tell that I was moving away from the creek.

I experienced a strange phenomenon for the first time when I got within one hundred feet of the ground. It's called "ground rush". At around this height, after you have descended from a higher altitude in a parachute, the ground suddenly starts to look like it is rushing up at you. I began to anticipate the impact. You are not supposed to do this because it can cause you to unintentionally "reach" for the ground with your feet. This can get your legs or ankles broken. The black hats know this and began yelling at all of us. I corrected just in time to do a pretty good parachute landing fall.

We were all moving slow after the shock of impact. This infuriated our instructors and we all got yelled at. I got quickly out of the harness after collapsing my chute. I put the harness into the kit bag, then quickly "S-folded" the chute and suspension lines and shoved them in on top of the harness. I snapped the reserve parachute onto the kit bag handles after zipping the bag shut and threw the entire kit onto my shoulders. I ran to the parachute turn-in point on the edge of the drop zone along with most of the other jumpers. We couldn't help noticing that some of our comrades were doing pushups in front of angry looking black hats who had apparently reached the conclusion that these guys were moving like slugs.

We turned in our chutes and climbed onto a truck that was soon rolling back toward the airfield at Ft. Benning. We would make one more jump that day, two more the next day, and one more the following evening. After that final jump, those of us who had made it through this short, but very difficult, school found ourselves standing in a formation on the edge of the drop zone. In that formation, we each received our coveted parachute wings one graduate at a time. Again, I realized that I had joined a very small brotherhood.

My friend Terry and I were in our newly acquired hot-rods the next day driving up Interstate 185 toward our new home in the 82nd Airborne Division at Ft. Bragg, NC. Our training would not end as long as we remained in the army. We would both endure even more difficult schools in the future. However, we were no longer "trainees". We were immature novice beginners to be sure, but as far as the army was concerned, we were now fully qualified infantry paratroopers. The US Army's 82nd Airborne Division was then and still is the finest light infantry division in the world. The dream job that I had longed for since sixth grade was right in front of me, but I was so immature that I had no idea how to handle it. We would soon discover that, even in the best regular army units at that time, there was a dark drug related subculture intent on ensnaring anyone foolish enough to get involved with it.

Chapter 6

Conflicted Patriot

"Behold, I stand at the door and knock.
If anyone hears my voice and opens the door,
I will come in to him and eat with him, and he with Me."
(Revelation 3:20)

I was assigned to A Company, 2nd Battalion, 325th Parachute Infantry Regiment from the 82nd Airborne Division replacement detachment. The 325th is also known as the 2nd Brigade. Terry was also assigned to the 325th, but our friends, Wayne and Max, were sent to the 504th Parachute Infantry Regiment, also known as the 3rd Brigade. We did some orientation training while we were in the replacement detachment. One of these training events involved doing a parachute jump from a seated position in the open door of a Bell Huey helicopter. I kind of liked this jump because the aircraft wasn't traveling as fast and it seemed like there was more time to react during the drop.

I finally reached my new company and learned that the unit was preparing to participate with the rest of the brigade in a very important field test exercise known as the ARTEP. This stands for Army Readiness Training Evaluation Program. The 82nd Airborne Division was a critical part of the US military's Rapid Deployment Force or "RDF". In order to be considered a "combat ready" part of the RDF, each of the involved army units had to successfully pass the evaluation standards embedded in the ARTEP. The entire division had to be certified as combat ready in order to remain part of the Rapid Deployment Force. For the 82nd Airborne Division, failure to qualify for this strategic role was not an option. This was a very important test. A great many military careers were in the balance.

I was quickly introduced to my new platoon leader, platoon sergeant, squad leader, and fire team leader. I learned that my squad was short handed and there were only two people in my fire team, myself and the team leader. I had not been home since I entered the army at the beginning of June. I was allowed to take a short leave of less than a week and went home for a few precious days.

I was immediately dragged into the frenzied preparation for this critical field exercise when I got back to the unit. I soon learned that here in this tough regular unit, I was very definitely a "new guy". The unit veterans diligently did everything they could to ensure that my initiation was thorough. One of my sergeants sent me down to the supply room on a particularly embarrassing "fool's errand" with instructions to sign out some "sky hooks". After getting laughed at and told that I had fallen for one of the older "stupid" gags, I determined not to be fooled the next time. I was being made to do a great deal of labor anyway as a private soldier in a fire team with no other privates. I was working in our platoon area a short while later when my new squad leader told me in a very serious voice to go down to the orderly room and get the keys to "Area J". I did as ordered and soon found myself getting laughed at again while someone explained that "Area J" was a designated training area shown on the maps of Ft. Bragg. They practically had to threaten me with bodily injury before I would do anything that in any way looked like it might be a prank after that.

The ARTEP started with a simulated combat parachute jump on a pitch black night from very low altitude. My squad leader insisted that I function as the door-man because this was my first jump with my new platoon. I would be the first person through the door on that side of the plane. The whole battalion, almost one thousand men, was going to jump in this "mass tactical" parachute drop. The C130 Hercules we were using was one of a great many identical planes in a huge staggered formation. The C130 is a large turbo prop cargo plane. It flies much slower than the C141. The required door position was the same position we learned on the 34 foot towers in jump school.

We were parachuting with almost all of the items we would carry if this jump had been into an actual combat situation. We had dry clothing and extra gear rolled up in our bedrolls which were crammed into waterproof containers called dry bags. These dry bags were attached to our parachute harnesses under the reserve parachutes. Our rifles were carried in cases attached vertically to the left sides of our harnesses. We were carrying all kinds of other items belt packs, shirt pockets, leg pockets, attached to our pistol belts, and clipped or taped to our shoulder straps. Each of us was carrying all kinds of stuff stashed anywhere we could find. The biggest trick was carrying everything we would need on the ground in a manner which ensured it would not come loose as we exited the aircraft. I could only imagine how much I weighed as I struggled to stand up and hook up.

The inside of the plane was illuminated with a red light to preserve our night vision. The night was extremely dark because there was no moon and the stars were obscured with high thin clouds. When I looked out through the doorway, it was like looking into a pool of ink. I had no idea what altitude we would be jumping at. I had only half listened to the ground briefing. I stood in the door in the body position I had learned in school with my knees bent, my hands holding the exterior of the doorway on both sides, and my eyes searching straight out for the invisible horizon.

The other men in my squad, which made up the first part of the stick, were right behind me in the door. A lot of them were yelling and carrying on as they waited for the word to go. When it came, I momentarily noticed a bright flash of green light and heard the word "Go!" I was up and out into that ink black night without any hesitation. My body position was bad again. I felt the twisted risers pushing my head forward and down when the parachute opened. I reached up and grabbed them, pulling them apart so that I could look up and check my canopy for blown sections or "gores". As I looked up, I realized that I might as well be blind. It was so pitch dark

I couldn't see anything. I pulled my head back down and started to kick in an effort to untwist the risers. Almost as soon as my eyes came back to level, I slammed into the ground with virtually no warning.

Escaping injury in that jump was another sign that God was protecting me, but I was too ignorant to appreciate it. I recovered, and quickly collapsed my parachute as I listened to plane after plane roar overhead. I could hear men landing all around me. I could also hear the sounds of a few small "unsecured" objects hitting the ground around me as they fell away from men exiting the low flying airplanes; so much for the brilliant idea of "stashing" things in your pockets.

A calculation based on our limited drift time tells me that we may have been as low as 500 feet when we made this jump. We were operating under very strict noise and light discipline and it took a while to regroup as a unit. The date of this jump was November 5, 1975. For the rest of that week, we worked our way through a very difficult field exercise that was intentionally made as realistic as possible.

I had already been introduced to marijuana by my squad mates. This was my first emersion into a world where well trained professional soldiers, considered to be among the best light infantry on the planet, did most of their patrolling and mission execution under the influence of marijuana and other more serious drugs. I wanted to be accepted. I caved in quickly even though I knew that what we were doing was dangerous and illegal. I was very young and a long way from home. I followed my fire team leader and did everything he did to the best of my ability.

One of my new barracks roommates was a young man named Chuck. Chuck played the harmonica so well that he soon landed a gig in a local blues band. He had a problem. The band wouldn't let him play on stage unless he could grow his hair out longer than the regulation GI haircut. He undoubtedly thought long and hard about the problem before coming up with what he thought was the perfect solution. He started using about a half bottle of hair oil on his head every morning before reporting for duty. As long as he kept the areas above his ears shaved, he could grow his hair out until it fell over his collar after he washed the oil out. One of the biggest problems with this stroke of genius was that, as part of our garrison uniform, we wore maroon felt berets. Chuck's beret soon took on a life of its own.

A normal day for Chuck would start with him reducing his long flowing hair to a grotesquely plastered mass before our first PT formation at 6:40AM. He would fight to stay distant from any senior authority figures throughout the duty day and then take a long shower to wash the oil out of his scalp right after he got off work. Changing into civilian clothes and an expensive leather jacket, he would breeze out of the barracks with his locks flowing out in glorious civilian blues-band harmonica player style. Anyone seeing him would never have mistaken him for an active duty soldier. This went on for some time before the inevitable dramatic confrontation between artistic license and military discipline shattered Chuck's dream of a career in music.

I was the door guard for the CQ that afternoon. It was still warm outside, and I was sitting at the top of the barracks steps enjoying the breeze. I saw the company first sergeant coming up the walk toward the stairs at about the same time I heard someone coming out of the barracks doorway behind me. It was Chuck, and he hadn't seen the first sergeant. There was nothing I could do to warn him. I sat there in suspended awe as Chuck simply trotted down the steps right past the first sergeant as if nothing was out of place. I heard the first sergeant say, "Good evening sir!" I didn't hear a reply from Chuck. He kept on walking briskly toward the end of the barracks sidewalk and the freedom beckoning from the parking lot beyond.

The first sergeant reached the top of the stairs and asked the CQ who the civilian was that had just walked out of the barracks. I didn't say a word. The CQ thought for a second and then realized who the first sergeant was talking about. He answered that it wasn't a civilian; it was a member of the unit. Chuck had almost made it to freedom. The next second, I was nearly deafened by the first sergeant roaring at Chuck and chasing him down with all of the compassionate fervor shown by a great white shark to a wounded baby seal. I couldn't say exactly what happened in the next several minutes, but the next time I saw Chuck his head was shaved; he had a new beret; and the post exchange had experienced a significant reduction in hair-oil sales.

The next couple of months in my new unit went by in a blur of training and inebriation. The training was intense and relentless. When we weren't working, we were stoned. As a matter of fact, we were often stoned while we were working. In a weird way, some of the training almost seemed more realistic when we were in that condition. This was especially true when we were patrolling at night and there was heavy use of pyrotechnics.

This pattern was interrupted for me one day while we were on a rather long field exercise that involved what the army called "reverse cycle training". In this type of training, you sleep during the day and do patrolling and range training at night. We had been out in the field for some time, and we were all pretty "ripe". It was early afternoon. I was sitting on the edge of the fox-hole that I shared with my fire team Leader. I probably should have been asleep, but I was wide awake for some reason. I heard a jeep drive up through the woods to the edge of our platoon defensive perimeter. When it stopped, I heard part of a subdued conversation between the driver of the jeep and my platoon sergeant. A few seconds later, the platoon sergeant shouted to my squad leader telling him that he needed a "volunteer" for a detail back in garrison.

My squad leader, of course, informed my fire team leader that I had just volunteered for the detail, what-ever it was. I was the new guy. That was just how it was. I was told to get all of my stuff together, throw it in the back of the jeep, and get in. I was soon on my way back to the barracks. I asked the driver what I was supposed to do when I got there. He told me to stow my stuff in my room and get to the battalion sergeant major's office as soon as possible. He didn't know what the detail was about, but he said I had to be there right away.

I didn't have time to clean up or change my uni-form. We had been patrolling in the woods overnight every night for days. My field uniform was filthy. I had camouflage paint over dirt over sweat faded camouflage paint covering my face, arms, and hands. I probably smelled almost as bad as the day I flew to New Orleans to visit Max's family, or worse. There was nothing I could do about it. I stashed my gear in the barracks and grabbed my beret. I don't remember what I was thinking as I ran across to the battalion headquarters building. I soon found myself standing before the desk of Command Sergeant Major Tom Fulton.

There were three other junior enlisted men in the room. They were all wearing Class A dress uniforms. I believe they were all either PFCs or specialist fours. The sergeant major asked me, in his gravelly voice, who I was. I gave him my name and rank and told him I had been sent over from A Company to report to him for a detail. He asked if I had been in the field for a while, and I said yes. He then dismissed the other men from the room and told me to stand at ease.

Looking me up and down, he announced that he thought I was just the candidate he had been looking for, a "real field trooper." Apparently the other young men in the Class A uniforms had also been candidates. They represented the other three sub units in the battalion, B Company, C Company, and the combat support company. Sergeant Major Fulton told me to go over and report to the brigade command sergeant major as soon as possible.

I walked into the brigade headquarters building after hastily getting cleaned up with a feeling of fear and awe. As I recall, I still didn't know what this was all about. Reporting to 2nd Brigade Command Sergeant Major Perry gave me a feeling eerily similar to the time I had to go to the principal's office in sixth grade. Apparently, he either liked what he saw in me or Sergeant Major Fulton had used his influence in a prior phone call. In any event, Sergeant Major Perry announced in his booming voice that I was just the young man he needed.

I soon learned that I would be transferred to the brigade headquarters company and that I was now the new driver and radio telephone operator for the brigade executive officer (XO), Lieutenant Colonel Frank Yon. What this meant in a practical sense was that I would drive whatever military vehicle Colonel Yon was using, and I would be responsible for his tactical electronic communications. I would be responsible for the operation and user level maintenance of his vehicle, radio equipment, encryption equipment, and code books when we were driving. I would carry and operate all of his backpack communication gear when we were traveling on foot. It meant that I would go to the field whenever he went to the field. I would be on every parachute jump he was on.

There were three generic airborne infantry battalions in each of the 82nd Airborne Division's three infantry brigades. When one of these brigades was deployed, it would have extra support and aviation units attached to it to form a regimental combat team. The division's RDF required that it was capable of inserting a significant combat ready force anywhere in the world within eighteen hours of the receipt of orders from the national command authority (the president of the United States).

The division's operational cycle at this time was divided into three segments or phases; Post Support (DRB 3), Training (DRB 2), and Mission phase (DRB 1). These phases lasted six weeks each. The brigade that had just completed a Mission phase would be stepped down to Post Support for six weeks. During Post Support, the troops in the brigade would be used as the name implies for support operations on Ft. Bragg. They would also be allowed to take personal leave during this phase. Generally speaking, the soldiers assigned to Post Support had to be able to return to Ft. Bragg in an emergency during this phase within 48 hours.

The brigade would enter the six week Training phase after Post Support. This phase was intended to provide intense training to sharpen their skills and combat readiness. During this phase, a lot of time was spent living in the field and training on ranges. Some soldiers also participated in exterior non-unit training schools during this phase, but most of them would be readily available for deployment within a day if needed.

The brigade would enter the six week Mission phase after completing the Training phase at the height of readiness. The units within the Mission phase DRB1 brigade were divided into Division Ready Force battalions known as DRF1, DRF2, and DRF 3. Each of the three infantry battalions within the brigade would cycle through two weeks in each of these three Division Ready Force assignments. The DRF 1 battalion had to be ready to deploy within two hours to any national or international military emergency. The DRF 2 and DRF 3 battalions were also ready to deploy within two hours but would be given sequentially lesser priorities for transportation than the DRF 1.

The three airborne infantry companies within the DRF 1 battalion would each take their cyclic turn forming what was called the Initial Deployment Force or IDF. The IDF had equipment pre-positioned at Pope Air Force

Base. They were ready to deploy within one hour of orders received from the president of the United States. These men, if ordered, would be the first boots on the ground anywhere in the world unless Marine Corps or special operations assets were more readily available.

This was very serious business. The Cold War was still in full insane swing. The United States and NATO were essentially involved in a long running stand-off for world domination with the Soviet Union, Warsaw Pact, and Chinese Peoples Republic. Although vastly superior in technology and industrial ability, the US and NATO were outnumbered, and we knew it. I know now that God was restraining the madness of the human race in it's bent toward mass suicidal world war.

The politicians at that time called it the "balance of power" between the super powers. It was also known as "Mutually Assured Destruction" or MAD. Simply put, Soviet nuclear weapons were aimed at our military and industrial sites. Our nuclear weapons were aimed at their cities. This precarious MAD balance was maintained for many years as we swayed ominously through small regional conflicts all over the planet. The 82nd Airborne Division was known as America's Guard of Honor. This meant that it had to be useable any where in the world along with several other key army, navy, air force, and marine units. We were to keep the fire from sparking in the first place if possible. We were to try and quickly stamp the fire out before humanity foolishly incinerated itself if prevention failed.

I now found myself in another new unit; brigade Headquarters Company or HHC. I shared a barracks room with the brigade commander's driver and RTO because of my assignment. We were both exempt from any police call (cleaning) or other support duties. I soon learned that my new boss, Lieutenant Colonel Yon, was a very active executive officer. Every time one of the battalions in the brigade made a parachute jump, we went with them. When one of the units was training in the field, we were there if possible.

Colonel Yon was physically a big man. He kind of reminded me of John Wayne. I looked up to him as a natural leader and a truly professional officer. I did my best to serve him as well as I possibly could. At the same time however, my drug and alcohol use had followed me to my new assignment, and I soon developed a miserable dual lifestyle. Like most of the other young men on Ft. Bragg in 1976, my life was strangely balanced between the driven world of a professional soldier and the manic pursuit of sex drugs and rock & roll.

Our work was important and we all knew it. Life was a strange mixture of long periods of lonely boredom punctuated by very interesting and often intensely dangerous events. We saw, heard, and did things at work on Ft. Bragg and other places that we would not have considered possible in our earlier civilian world. I can safely say that most of us just wanted to get out and go home. It was easy to fall into a wild hedonistic lifestyle when it was shared with so many other young men who felt themselves trapped in the same situation. This attitude seemed to be shared by the majority of the junior enlisted soldiers in the army at that time even in legendary units like the 82nd Airborne Division.

The war in Vietnam had recently ended. The US culture at large seemed like it had been taken over by a "hippy" mentality of free sex, prolific drug use, and rock music. There was an unreasonable and irrational sense that "we" had lost the war in Vietnam. The American people were tired of war. There was very little respect shown to the US military in the mid 70s. The culture had changed dramatically. Most of us realized that the army we belonged to was not the same as the army we heard about when we were children.

Many young Americans were caught up in a wave of anti-authority backlash and quickly became enmeshed in a bizarre counter-culture. The army at that time was made up of a cross section of the society at large. It was a very dark period in our national history. There were some soldiers, even then, that had decided to make the army a career. These young men were quickly labeled as "lifers" and socially ostracized by the majority of the members of almost every regular line unit. The "cool" people were just as quickly labeled "heads". If you were cool you were accepted. If you were a lifer you were tolerated but never fully trusted.

The drug subculture was so powerful in the army in those days, that it was possible to walk through the hallway of a military police barracks on any given Saturday night and smell a thick odor of marijuana smoke. The army hierarchy clearly didn't know what to do about the problem. In fact, the army leadership probably made the situation worse by continuing to allow, and in some cases encouraging, the prolific use of alcohol. To the young soldiers of that day, any diligent effort to control drug abuse seemed pretty hypocritical while the army leadership allowed beer vending machines in the barracks. The army had numerous officer/NCO club facilities on every post. These were nothing less than government owned night clubs. This was a confusing time for everyone, and the army didn't yet have an effective method for drug testing their personnel. The strict service discipline quickly broke down in the polluted subculture which had its own strict (though unwritten) rules and code of secrecy. I am not defending either side of this equation. It is my simple observation, as one who served during this time, that after the debacle in Vietnam, the United States Army took several years to sort through the quagmire of cultural and moral issues it was burdened with.

It was only after many difficult years that the army managed to shake these issues off and once again become the solid professional fighting force that it is today. I was in it. I was involved at the sharp end of the spear during this time. I firmly believe we would have been able to perform as an effective combat force if the need had arisen. However, I also believe that our country should be very grateful to God that nothing happened to significantly test our ability as a fighting force during the period of 1975 through 1978.

I was simultaneously involved in two very different lifestyles during this difficult period. Sergeant Major Perry was soon replaced as the brigade command sergeant major by Sergeant Major Fulton. Sergeant Major Fulton had been in the military for about thirty years. My duty hours were now usually spent working either directly for Colonel Yon, or for Sergeant Major Fulton.

I quickly became expert in the use and maintenance of the colonel's communication equipment through application and sheer necessity. I often found myself in strange company as I became one of those shadowy, less significant, junior service personnel that always surround important military officials and senior officers. I became very familiar with almost all of the members of the headquarters staff. This familiarity was necessary, but it was not good for me in my immature mindset. I was often in very close proximity to very important officers and overheard many conversations that would normally have been restricted to personnel far above my pay grade. Ironically, I remained trustworthy with those secrets. I treated these type secrets in virtually the same way I treated secrets regarding the criminal drug trade that I was also intimately familiar with.

Military leadership and tactical application were and still are fascinating subjects to me. I always have been interested in history. During this time in my life, I found myself exposed to events and circumstances that could potentially become historic. I was excited to be a part of it. While I was at work, I did the best I could to perform my duties well. My immaturity did get me in trouble a few times, and some of the embarrassingly stupid things I did should mercifully be left in the past. When I was off duty, I spent every waking moment and all of the money I had chasing women, looking for the next drug buzz, and partying in search of mindless oblivion. This went on for almost three years.

Not every adventure during this time in my life was dark or illegal. I progressed in pay grade over the next year and a half to specialist four (E4). I had become pretty good at doing what the army had assigned me to do. On the range, I became very good with my individual weapons. As part of my military duties, I spent a lot of time in the field at Ft. Bragg and other army installations.

I lost track of the number of jumps I had made after several months. I had the opportunity to parachute from almost every model of air force fixed wing cargo plane and army cargo helicopter in use during that time.

Life was a blur for me. I saw some humor in almost everything, but I was still distinctly aware of the serious physical and legal danger I was in much of the time. One of my friends in the headquarters company was a young American Samoan named Fiji. Fiji was one of the vehicle mechanics that worked in the brigade motor pool. Fiji was a great mechanic. He was also one of those people who are naturally gifted with tremendous physical strength. Fiji spoke good English, but with a thick Samoan accent. He was always quick to laugh, and a great friend when you were in trouble.

Our three story cinder block barracks was just one among many identical buildings laid out row after row in the 82nd Airborne Division garrison area. The unit that occupied the barracks across the courtyard from ours was an airborne infantry line company from the 2nd battalion, 325th PIR. Many of the non-infantry members of the headquarters company often referred to the infantrymen as "line dogs", "line doggies", or just "doggies". The infantrymen in turn had their own choice set of descriptive labels for the "rear echelon" personnel occupying "unnecessary" duty positions in the headquarters company. I was an infantryman that happened to be a member of the headquarters company. As such, I made it a personal policy to stay out of and as far away from the interactions between these two groups as possible.

One night this infantry company had returned from a long field training exercise. They were busily cleaning up and stowing all of their equipment when someone from Headquarters Company began shooting bottle rockets at them from across the courtyard. The infantrymen returned fire from their side of the courtyard using the last of their military issue star clusters and parachute flares. There were probably several other things launched or thrown between the buildings before the confrontation settled down into a rough stalemate, but I don't remember.

I was sleeping in my barracks room later that night when I heard someone beating on my door. I got up and yanked the door open to see that the hallway was full of a dense cloud of white smoke. A hand and arm shot into my room from the wall of smoke holding a gas mask. I heard a muffled voice yelling at me to put on the mask and evacuate the building immediately. Not knowing what was going on, I put on the mask and groped my way to the stairwell, down to the first floor, and out to the courtyard. A large group of my comrades were huddled close together in the yard coughing, spitting, and trying to figure out what was going on.

The fire department had just arrived and they were busily setting up their equipment. Suddenly, there was a loud crashing noise at the orderly room end of the building. We soon saw a very angry, bloody, and battered Fiji come running toward us from that direction across the yard. He was yelling almost unintelligibly and had to be physically restrained from assaulting anyone he thought might be responsible for what had happened. A few moments earlier, he had gotten the same knock on his door that I had. Unfortunately, he either wasn't given a gas mask, or he didn't put it on before trying to get out of the barracks.

We lived on the third floor. Fiji found himself running down the barracks hallway almost totally blinded by smoke and unable to breathe. He couldn't find the door to the stairwell and actually fell over the CQ table causing it to collapse. Panic set in, and he ran the length of the building before he found an open door at the opposite end. Running through that room, Fiji forced the window open and jumped out. He fell two stories to the roof of the orderly room below and landed on the tar and gravel covering the roof. Rolling over as he landed, he fell off that roof to the ground below. As I already described, he was a bloody mess, although amazingly, he wasn't seriously injured. He was a very angry Samoan.

We soon found out that someone had deposited a live white smoke grenade in each of the two stairwells on the ground floor. The smoke had naturally traveled upward and filled the top floor. It didn't require Sherlock Holmes and Dr. Watson to figure out who the culprits were. Needless to say, no "line doggies" were safe around Fiji after that.

Several of my friends and I decided to drive out to the woods one Sunday afternoon to build a bonfire and have a party. We found what we thought was a good spot in the forest near the old 82nd Airborne Division area between the perimeter of Ft. Bragg and the adjoining perimeter of Pope Air Force Base. There were probably eight or nine of us out there with my Mustang and another car. We had a pretty good fire going when we saw two sets of headlights coming toward us through the trees. The lights got to within thirty yards or so and stopped. We heard someone yelling at us over loud speakers. We moved through the trees to investigate and realized that the lights were from two air force security police pickup trucks that were facing us from the other side of a tall chain link fence. Even in our inebriated condition, we concluded that the security police couldn't get to us because there was no gate in the fence. They had obviously been sent to see what the source of the fire was near the base perimeter.

We believed ourselves to be unassailable at first. We began throwing beer cans and obscenities at the security personnel from our side of the fence. Suddenly, one of the brilliant members of our party observed that the security police on the air force side of the fence had radios that could talk with the army military police on our side of the fence. Without stopping to put out the fire, we jumped into the two cars and drove toward the highway. I had five people in my car. As we entered the garrison area, we began seeing flashing blue lights on the tops of several military police jeeps converging toward us.

I decided that there was no way I was going to be caught by military police personnel driving jeeps that were unable to exceed 45mph. I drove like a maniac through the close streets of the division area and out onto Longstreet Road. We soon suspected that military police sedans would be involved in the chase as well. I cut through a post housing area to the back side of the new 82nd Airborne Division garrison. We found ourselves roaring across the back of the Post Exchange bowling-alley parking lot and onto the back parking lot of our own 2nd brigade headquarters building. I jumped the curb with the car and did a long wheel spinning sweep across the grassy side yard of our headquarters and out onto the front parking lot. From there, we thundered out onto the next street and turned up a side street between rows of barracks buildings.

We realized that the best place to hide anything is right in front of the people searching. I pulled the car into the parking lot that served the 82nd Airborne Division headquarters building. I parked the car between two other vehicles. We were now quite sober. We got out, locked the car, and walked quickly away. The car sat in that parking space for several days.

The next morning was Monday. As my duty day started, I was being addressed by a furious Sergeant Major Fulton. He marched me out and showed me the giant trenches that had been torn in "his" headquarters grass yard. He gave me all kinds of inside information regarding what he would do to whoever was responsible for this, if he ever caught them. He then made me go get a shovel and do my best to repair the damaged yard. It was quite a bit of work fixing that torn up grass. I think now that, although justice wasn't fully served, it wasn't an accident that I was the one out there fixing what I had torn up.

I decided many days later to get my car off post before someone found it. The car was unique and very noticeable. It had virtually no mufflers on the exhaust system and was extraordinarily loud. I walked over to the division headquarters parking lot one afternoon at the end of the duty day and started the motor. I drove out of the lot and headed for one of the many post exits. I hadn't gotten far when I saw a military police jeep right behind me with a flashing blue light on top. I pulled over to the side of the street and waited with fearful anticipation as the military policeman walked up to the driver's side window.

The MP asked for my driver's license and ID card. I handed them out the window to him. He studied them for a moment before handing them back. He then told me that my car was entirely too loud to be driven on Ft. Bragg. I told him I was just in the process of taking it off post. He told me not to bring the car back on post until the exhaust was fixed. I thanked him and drove away. I never did bring the car back on post. I ended up selling it not long after this. All things considered, selling it was probably the smartest thing I ever did with that Mustang. Again, God was protecting me even in my rebellion.

I drove Colonel Yon to Sicily Drop Zone on Ft. Bragg one day to observe a mass tactical parachute drop that was being conducted by one of the battalions in our brigade. I had been on many of these drops myself. I thought I knew what to expect. There's a great deal of difference in perspective between someone participating in this type of operation and someone watching it from the edge of the drop zone. We were sitting in the jeep near a paved area that included a small set of bleachers used by dignitaries and others during airborne demonstrations.

An observer can't help being impressed by the power and magnitude of what is happening as large cargo planes approach the drop zone in a staggered formation. The noise grows to a muffled roar as the planes cross the initial release point and heavy drop platforms with vehicles and equipment are ejected and slowed in their descent to the ground via three or more giant parachutes each. The next aircraft in the formation follow with hundreds of paratroopers. Within seconds, the troops begin to fill the sky in stick after stick of OD green parachutes.

Colonel Yon and I were sitting there with the engine running while we watched on this particular day. Everything seemed to be going very well when two of the parachutists suddenly collided in mid air. They were about 100 feet off the ground when the accident happened. One of the parachutes immediately collapsed. The other chute partially collapsed in what was euphemistically referred to as a "cigarette roll". Both troopers plummeted to earth with only the slight wind drag of that partially collapsed chute to slow them down. They hit the ground right next to each other on the other side of the drop zone from where we were sitting in the jeep.

A tactical ambulance started screaming across the drop zone toward them swerving to miss the scattered jumpers who were spread out everywhere. Colonel Yon and I were right behind the ambulance. When we got to within a short distance, I stopped the jeep. We jumped out and ran the rest of the way. One of the men was screaming in a blood curdling way that will be hard to ever forget. Even more terrifying, the other soldier wasn't making a sound. Both men were still alive. The man who was screaming had a crushed pelvis and other injuries. The other man had a broken back. They were evacuated to Womack Army Hospital, and both survived. This incident didn't do anything to make me less fearful when jumping out of airplanes. It did remind me of my own mortality. For a short time, I probably even cleaned up my behavior.

I continued to grow stronger in my knowledge of radio communications and crypto equipment through prolonged and intense field experience. At the same time, I continued to participate in airborne operations at every opportunity. I don't know how many parachute jumps I made in this duty position, but on one occasion, I managed to make three jumps in one day from a Bell Huey helicopter on St. Mere Eglise Drop Zone.

Several junior members of the brigade headquarters staff and I were sitting around on fallen logs in the woods eating breakfast early one morning during a field training exercise. We were surrounded by concertina wire and large tactical tents with camouflage netting. We heard someone approaching, and looked up to see a perplexed looking Fiji walking up to join us. As Fiji sat down on the log, someone asked him what was bothering him. Listening to Fiji tell a story was often similar to watching or reading a cartoon. He was one of the best mechanics in the brigade motor pool, and he had tremendous physical strength. Fiji was always colorful and naturally very funny. As he sat there eating his breakfast, he explained that he had been working most of the night on one of the six wheeled semi amphibious "Gama Goat" trucks that had been damaged somehow during the previous day's operations. During the wee hours of the morning while it was still very dark, Fiji had concluded that he could not complete the repairs in the field and decided to take the vehicle back to the garrison motor pool facilities. The vehicle could be driven, but just barely.

Fiji went on to explain, "I drove out through da wire and onto da trail usin the black-out drive lights... I could hardly see anythin... I's drivin along da trail an I see up ahead a ways... a log in da road... I says to myself, Fiji, you could jus drive right over dat log in dis Goat.... den I says, no Fiji, da Goat's busted... ya go drivin over logs in da road an ya jus make it worse... He kind of paused for a few seconds, and somebody had to ask, "Well what happened then?" Fiji got a strange look on his face and continued, "Well, I stops da Goat, an I climbs out, and I walks up to move da log... When I starts ta pick it up, I find it aint a log at all... it a man in a sleepin bag!!" He paused again until somebody had to ask him what he did next. He said, "Well, I reach down, pick up dat man... an I chuck him off into da bushes!! Den I gits back in da Goat and goes on bout my bidness..." We were all laughing so hard we barely heard anything else he said about the damaged Gama Goat.

There was a large parachute operation planned for our brigade one day on Holland Drop Zone at the far end of Ft. Bragg. I drove Colonel Yon to the airborne liaison office at Pope Air Force Base so that he could check on the operation from the air force perspective. He soon learned that something was wrong. Before the drop could be executed, the weather and ground wind speed had to be verified in person by the drop zone safety officer (DZSO). The DZSO in this case was not reachable via radio. He had not been seen or heard from since he had gone out to the drop zone a few hours earlier. I have no idea how many millions of dollars were being wasted in aviation fuel by this time, but Colonel Yon decided that the only thing to do was to drive out and find the hapless DZSO as soon as possible. This was a pretty long drive in an open jeep at a top speed of 45mph accompanied by a senior officer with the patience of a ticking time bomb.

Holland drop zone is located at the far end of Ft. Bragg, about twenty miles from the garrison area and Pope Air Force Base. This was the largest drop zone on Ft. Bragg. A large urban mock-up training area has since been added to this drop zone, but back then it had rolling sand dunes and looked a lot like old pictures of the Sahara desert. When we got there, we drove all over the place looking for the DZSO with no success. We then began driving around the outside of the drop zone in an expanding search pattern on various dirt roads and fire breaks. We finally spotted the DZSO's jeep stopped quite some distance from the drop zone. He was leaning over the back of the vehicle working frantically on his radio system. Colonel Yon made me stop our jeep about thirty yards short of the young lieutenant's vehicle.

He silently jumped out and strode up to the frightened and miserable junior officer in fiery "John Wayne" style. I couldn't tell what was being said, but I could recognize a solid chewing when I saw one. After almost a minute of this, Colonel Yon stomped back to our jeep and jumped in. Without looking at me, he told me to get out and go fix the young lieutenant's radio for him. As I walked up to the other jeep, I could see that the lieutenant was in terrible distress. I really felt sorry for him as I asked how I could help. He told me that he couldn't find the drop zone and that he couldn't get his radio to work.

I told him that the drop zone was just a short distance away and gave him the direction. I was tempted to add that it would be kind of hard to miss, being the only huge terrain feature in the area that resembled the Sahara desert, but I thought better of it. As I looked at the lieutenant's radio set, I found that it was on the correct frequency but it was adjusted to an incorrect squelch setting. I flipped the switch and corrected the problem. I went on to act like I was doing other things to the radio and told the lieutenant to track with me so that he wouldn't look as bad to the colonel. He worked with me and we spent a couple of quick minutes while I tried to encourage him and help him get his bearings straight.

I then asked him do a communications check on his radio with the range control office and walked back to the colonel's jeep. As the lieutenant sped off toward the drop zone, I jumped back behind the wheel next to Colonel Yon and started the engine. He very calmly said "the squelch was set wrong, wasn't it?" I said "yes sir". He said something else about green lieutenants, and we drove quietly back to Ft. Bragg while the airborne operation went on behind us.

Eventually I was moved into the position of driver and RTO for the brigade commander. After I had been in that job for several months, the Army finally began active drug testing. Sergeant Major Fulton found out that I indeed had a problem although he never really said anything directly to me about it.

Our brigade participated in a large training exercise on Eglin Air Force Base in Florida at about this same time. During this twelve day trip, two brigades of the 24th Infantry Division were pitted against the 2nd Brigade of the 82nd Airborne Division. As the driver and RTO for the 2nd Brigade commander, I was given a "front row seat" for many of the discussions between the senior officers in these involved units. The 82nd Airborne Division and the 24th Infantry Division were both part of the 18th Airborne Corps at that time.

The senior officers involved in viewing and participating in this exercise included the 18th Airborne Corps Commander, both division commanders, and all three brigade commanders. It was interesting when the commander of the 24th asked the corps commander to stop the exercise after two days so that the "sides" could be reset. The implication was that he wanted the corps commander to force the troopers from the 82nd to give all of the stuff back that they had taken from the men and units of the 24th. It was a reminder that the 82nd was a very different kind of unit.

The design and primary mission of the 82nd Airborne Division was to interdict the frontal edge of battle area (FEBA), create chaos in the enemy rear, and force the enemy to redirect combat assets to secure their interior supply and communication lines. Our troopers were simply doing their jobs and doing them very well. Somehow this didn't seem fair to the regular "leg" infantry units of the 24th. It didn't occur to our men that they were outnumbered 2-1. The 82nd Airborne Division is still that kind of unit. That's why it has been used strategically as a force multiplier since it was reorganized as an airborne division during WWII. This "swashbuckling pirate-like" reputation was one of the characteristics that appealed to my immature mindset and drew me to the unit in the first place. It was also very dangerous because it fit well with my perceptions of my own illegal personal behavior.

I was confronted one night during this exercise by a very angry Sergeant Major Fulton who was shining his red-lensed flashlight into my eyes and asking me if I was "high". I had left a weapon and a sensitive encryption keying device in the colonel's vehicle between the seats and had stepped about ten yards away from the vehicle to get some chow. There was vegetation between me and the vehicle which kept it from being in my direct line of sight. The headquarters company commander had walked past the vehicle in the darkness and discovered my indiscretion. He had removed these two very sensitive items from the vehicle and turned them over to the Command sergeant major.

Sergeant Major Fulton was understandably furious. He gave me one of the most intense and "artistic" tail chewings I had received in quite some time. I deserved it. He was absolutely right. I couldn't help wondering even then about his reference to me being "high". I wasn't high thankfully, but I believe he knew from my drug tests that it was a possibility.

Not long after returning from this exercise, I was sent to the Primary Non-Commissioned Officers Course in preparation for a possible future promotion to sergeant E5. This school was all about leadership in a combat environment. We were taught everything from leading physical training exercises to leading combat and reconnaissance patrols. We learned how to effectively conduct performance oriented training classes, and how to supervise soldiers at the squad level. We were taught to construct and deliver properly organized patrol warning and operation orders. We were then taught how to lead those patrols in the field. All this classroom training was backed up with what seemed like endless practical application in the woods of the Spring Lake Training Area near Ft. Bragg. The cadre members and instructors in this school were almost exclusively infantry combat veteran sergeants. The basic leadership training I received at this school was probably the best I received in my entire military career. This could possibly have also been affected by the fact that I was away from illicit drugs for the entire length of the course.

I continued to do my job in brigade headquarters for several months after returning from the NCO academy until I was transferred to a new anti-armor company. It was now early autumn 1977. The Soviet Union and Warsaw Pact nations had a combined armor strength that included a staggering 50,000 tanks. Many of these tanks were antiquated armored relics from WWII and the 1950s, but they were still tanks. They were still functional and potentially lethal armored vehicles. Most of them were positioned near the border between East and West Germany. All of the NATO countries combined could only field about 20,000 tanks, and a great many of these were physically located inside the continental United States. At this point in the Cold War, there was a very real concern that the Soviets and their allies might charge over the German border suddenly. Strategic planners feared that they could seize West Germany with this giant armored force, before NATO could do anything to stop them without using tactical nuclear weapons.

This led to the development of anti-armor infantry units which would deploy along with other rapid deployment forces. Strategic and tactical planners had understood since WWI that the best weapon to use against infantry was the main battle tank. The opposite was also a well understood truth. The best weapon that could be used to stop and destroy tanks was well equipped infantry.

The United States and our NATO allies developed several very effective anti-armor infantry weapons during the late decades of the Cold War. In the mid 1970s, each infantry battalion in the 82nd Airborne Division had a TOW anti-armor platoon consisting of three sections of two squads each. Each of these TOW squads operated a TOW anti tank missile launcher. TOW, or more correctly TOWATGM, stands for "Tube launched Optically tracked Wire command link Anti-Tank Guided Missile". The TOW weapon system was first developed during the Vietnam War and then improved upon in many ways over the next decade. It is a very powerful, extraordinarily accurate, easily mobile weapon system.

The weapon was used mostly as a "bunker buster" in Vietnam because the enemy in that conflict was rarely protected by armor. In 1977, we learned that the army had decided to add entire TOW companies with three anti-armor platoons each to all three of the infantry brigades in the 82nd Airborne Division. This was a much needed anti-armor reinforcement to the army's only light airborne infantry division assigned to the RDF in view of the massive Soviet armor threat. These new companies would be designated as Echo Companies and assigned directly to each brigade command. In our case, the new company was Echo Company, 325th Parachute Infantry Regiment or E/325.

I was encouraged by Sergeant Major Fulton, among others, to volunteer for reassignment to this new unit. This gave me the unusual experience of joining a brand new military organization as a cadre member while it was being formed. I was still a specialist 4 (E4). The army had effectively stopped using the corporal (E4) rank many years earlier. However, I was needed to fill a sergeant E5 NCO position. Since I was still an E4, the army simply converted me from specialist to corporal and I was reassigned to the unit.

I moved to a new barracks once again and found myself involved with a new set of total strangers. I brought my dubious double lifestyle of drug and alcohol abuse punctuated by sober periods of professional soldiering to this new unit. I was no longer responsible for just one person however. I was now expected to effectively lead a small squad of four men who would deploy and operate a very valuable and critically important weapon system. I had reached the ripe old age of 20.

Chapter 7

Recalcitrant Professional

"if you confess with your mouth that Jesus is Lord and believe in your heart that God raised Him from the dead, you will be saved. For with the heart one believes and is justified, and with the mouth one confesses and is saved."
(Romans 10:9, 10)

I soon discovered that my company was made up of a diverse collection of new soldiers from the division replacement detachment and older personnel from several other units within the 82nd Airborne Division. Several of the junior officers were brand new 2nd lieutenants. The company commander and the first sergeant had, until recently, worked together in the brigade S2 (Intelligence) office. The rest of the company noncommissioned officers were almost exclusively sergeants with solid experience in anti-armor tactics generally, and the TOW weapon system specifically. I was a freshly minted corporal. Although I had been trained on the Dragon weapon system, I knew very little at first about the larger TOW missile. The remaining enlisted personnel were mostly brand new privates fresh from Jump School at Ft. Benning. We also received some experienced soldiers from the recently deactivated 17th Cavalry Regiment. The army required that this diverse group of people be transformed into a cohesive combat ready unit within one year. The platoons would be attached as "strap hangers" to the individual battalions within the brigade and used at each battalion commander's discretion if deployment became necessary before the end of that year. The international strategic circumstances had demanded the creation of these new units. These circumstances did not allow for a year of preparation. The crash course started immediately.

My new platoon leader was a fairly weak 2nd lieutenant. My new platoon sergeant was a straight laced family man that cared deeply about his mission. The three section leaders and two other squad leaders were experienced noncommissioned officers. In fact, two of them were Vietnam combat veterans. I was one of the three squad leaders. The platoon leader, as new officers often do, tried to lead in an authoritarian manner at first. The platoon sergeant focused much of his attention as needed on training the lieutenant to balance his authority and actions to get the best results from his subordinate leaders and men.

The other noncommissioned officers soon lost respect for both the platoon leader and the platoon sergeant although they avoided any open display of disrespect. I quickly learned that all of the subordinate noncommissioned officers in my platoon smoked pot. They all had the same strange double life that I had. I was immediately adopted by all of them as a little brother. It is very difficult to explain the strange dichotomy here. These sergeants were technically and tactically proficient with the complicated weapon systems and crucially important small units they led. They were functional experts in their specific military specialty. At the same time, they displayed a level of nonmilitary disrespect for the army hierarchy that, from a military perspective, seemed like moral bankruptcy. Sadly, I fit right in.

We had trained within a few months to the point where each of the sections and squads performed their tactical functions with almost machine like precision. The platoon struggled as a whole for obvious reasons. The platoon leader and platoon sergeant didn't always stay with us as we trained in the field. In fact, they rarely did. Most of our training was conducted at the section and squad level with the sections only interacting as needed. On one occasion, we were encamped in an administrative platoon bivouac near Normandy Drop Zone on Ft. Bragg. We had been doing station to station training for days.

I was supervising a station in which I taught the new troops how to construct a firing position "range card". A range card was needed any time a crew served weapon was employed in a fixed position. The card was hand drawn. It showed critical terrain features, pre-plotted artillery targets, relative elevations, alternate positions, friendly locations, and relative ranges or distances. I had meticulously constructed a sand table model of a battlefield. I was using the sand table to teach the troops what features had to be included as they drew their range cards. I was pretty proud of this training station and steadily improved my own ability to draw range cards as I instructed others on the subject.

I found myself getting bored one day as the troops circulated from station to station and my audience grew steadily smaller. I soon found myself with no audience at all. I walked away from the range card station in search of something else to do. I came across a copperhead snake stretched out on a log in the sun as I strolled through the pine woods. I killed the snake and picked it up with a forked stick. This seemed like a great opportunity for entertainment as I walked through the woods searching for a victim. I soon heard the voice of one of my close friends, Sergeant Snow, drifting through the trees and bushes out in front of me. Sergeant Snow, a young black E5, was always quick to laugh and amazingly positive. He was a great friend. He was also deathly afraid of snakes.

I realized that I was actually approaching his open air classroom from behind him and in front of the class as I made my way through the foliage. About twenty soldiers were sitting on logs in a semi circle facing Sergeant Snow. He had an actual wooden lectern that he was using to hold his notes and papers as he gave a spirited lecture to the class. I broke cover behind him and immediately gained the rapt attention of all of his students. I walked quietly up to his side and laid the snake on the lectern in front of him while asking what kind of snake it was. Sergeant Snow gave a less than manly shriek and ran like a rabbit. I had to finish delivering his class after everyone stopped laughing. For some reason, it took him a long time to completely forgive me and let that one go.

The TOW missile launchers we had at that time could either be ground mounted on tripods, or vehicle mounted in the bed of specially designed open top jeeps. Part of the training plan we had been given required the troops to participate in vehicle mounted land navigation training using these jeeps. Some of this navigation training was supposed to be conducted at night under black-out conditions.

A combat engineer unit had been operating in the same area, unfortunately, the week before we attempted to do this training. The engineers had dug several pit style tank traps along the fire breaks that were used essentially as dirt roads by people like us. Contrary to post regulations and plain common sense, the engineers had failed to fill in all of these tank traps at the end of their training. The remaining pits filled with water from very heavy rain. We failed to conduct a thorough reconnaissance of the entire area before the start of our navigation training. The existence of the tank traps went unnoticed until all of them were found "the hard way" on the first night of our exercise. Several vehicles were severely damaged, but miraculously no one was injured. I believe this may have been the first time our platoon leader received any special attention from our company commander.

We spent so much time in the field training and preparing for potential conflict with a large armored force that we eventually began to develop new ideas regarding tactical survival in the expected environment. If the worst case occurred, we wanted to engage enemy tanks from maximum range and from the flanks or rear if possible. We came up with elaborate plans for hide positions, and for masking our missile launches with smoke or intentionally detonated explosives out on our flanks. We requested high power sniper rifles for our sections (although we never got them) with the idea that a sniper could shoot a tank commander or two from a hidden position and force all the tanks in a formation to close their hatches or "button up". This would partially blind them by forcing them to rely on their periscope systems rather than observing from open tank hatches. We planned different kinds of ambush tactics, as well as use of various tank traps and improvised munitions.

Our expectation was that if we were called on to slow the potential armored advance into Western Europe, we would be dropped into the mess with little possibility of resupply or reinforcement. I think we all understood that if something like this happened, NATO would use us as little more than a strategic speed bump to slow the Soviets down and allow a better prepared response. I also believe that we all thought we would somehow survive this kind of disaster. We trained vigorously with our crew served weapons, field craft, and escape and evasion techniques. We dug vehicle and squad size fighting positions all over Ft. Bragg. We cut down a great many huge pine trees to construct overhead cover reinforced by enough packed earth to withstand direct hits from large artillery shells.

Our entire company was eventually assigned a training day on the Claymore mine range. The Claymore is a deadly effective anti personnel mine. It consists of a curved rectangular plastic box filled with a pound and a half of C4 explosive and over 700 steel ball bearings. Properly emplaced, it stands on short metal legs with the outward side of the curve facing toward the expected enemy. The mine is detonated with an electronic blasting cap that is inserted in the top of the device while it is being positioned. A wire is strung back to the friendly position foxhole where it is connected to a squeeze type handheld electric pulse generator that we euphemistically called the "clacker". In NCO academy, I had been taught how to connect a lot of these mines to an army field telephone switch-board by a Vietnam veteran cadre member. He had used this method to great effect when defending his fire base from a Viet Cong night attack several years earlier.

My platoon was tasked by our company commander with operation of this range for the rest of the company that day. My platoon leader was to be the Officer In Charge (OIC) of the range. One of my very close friends, a staff sergeant named Irvin, was the Non-Commissioned Officer In Charge (NCOIC). Irvin was a highly decorated Vietnam War hero veteran of the 173rd Regimental Combat Team. I don't remember where our regular platoon sergeant was at that time, but Irvin was the acting platoon sergeant that day. All of the other sergeants in the platoon would act as lane supervisors on the firing line. I was assigned as the ammunition point supervisor.

This range was laid out like many of the firing ranges on almost every US Army post. It had a driveway leading up to it from the main road. There was a tall flag pole stationed at the intersection with a red flag flying to indicate that the range was in use. The firing line was positioned on the forward slope of a hill. The hill crest blocked direct line of sight from the main road. There was a large double set of bleachers located behind the firing line at a safe enough distance to allow observation of events on the line. A range control tower with a loud public address system stood above the bleachers. Latrine facilities were positioned directly behind the bleachers. The ammunition disbursement point was located behind and to the side of the bleachers at a safe distance from the firing line.

The firing line on this range consisted of a long row of commercially constructed "foxholes" lined with huge sections of concrete sewer pipe buried in the ground vertically. The holes were deep enough so that a man of average height could stand up in the hole with his head and shoulders sticking out. In front of these holes, each position had a time-warn path leading about 25 meters forward onto the range. A small dirt berm at the end of this path marked the spot where the mines were supposed to be deployed. Way out beyond this point, several hundred meters, were some ancient armored vehicles that served as targets when the range was used to train on other weapon systems.

The ammunition disbursement point consisted of a three sided low concrete wall that was just the right size to hold a standard jeep trailer. This wall was obviously intended to cause any accidental explosion of stacked ammunition to expend its force upward. It also served to protect the ammunition from ricochets or other pro-jectiles coming from the impact area of the range.

We were on the range early that morning. Irvin and the platoon leader had driven to the post ammunition storage facility even earlier and signed for our allotment of a large number of Claymore mines packed in several cases. These cases were stacked inside the ammo point wall when the rest of the company soldiers and noncommissioned officers arrived by 2 ½ ton truck. All of the troops were ordered into the bleachers where one of our sergeants gave them a refresher training lecture on the proper deployment and use of the mine.

The soldiers were then ordered to wait in the bleachers for their turn to file up to the ammunition disbursement point. When they got there, I would issue each of them a cloth bandolier containing one Claymore mine, two blasting caps, a one hundred foot spool of electric wire, a mine test module, and a "clacker". After receiving this equipment, they would be escorted down onto the firing line and turned over to our other sergeant's who were acting as lane supervisors at each of the firing line foxholes.

The soldiers would then crawl out onto the range from the foxholes along the paths to the emplacement positions where they would set up and connect their individual mines. Crawling back to the foxholes, they would connect the other end of the lines to the testing modules and connect the testing modules to the clackers. When everyone was ready, our lieutenant, speaking over the PA system from the control tower, would order all of the troops on the line to take cover and test their mines. The clackers were all squeezed at the same time while the operators watched a small test light on the module to confirm that the clackers were producing an electric spark.

The soldiers were then ordered to remove the test modules and reconnect the clackers directly to the lines. After ensuring that the firing line was clear and everyone on it was under cover, the lieutenant ordered everyone on the line to detonate their mines. This was followed by a huge ragged explosion involving the dispersion of thousands of ball bearing projectiles in front of the firing line. The troops were then ordered out of the foxholes and told to police up their debris before being escorted off the firing line.

This went on group after group for over an hour. There was still one case of mines left in the ammunition disbursement point after every soldier in the company had detonated one mine. Each case contained nine bandoliers and nine mines. The whole company was now sitting in the bleachers "smoking and joking" while they waited for the trucks to return to the range and drive them back to the barracks.

I was sitting on the parapet wall of the ammunition disbursement point talking with the platoon medic when our platoon leader walked up with Irvin and the rest of our platoon noncommissioned officers. I told them that there was one case of mines left. A discussion ensued regarding what to do with them. The lieutenant wanted to return the case intact to the ammunition storage facility. Irvin pointed out that the ammo facility didn't like to take any ammunition back and would demand a great deal of paperwork and hassle before they accepted it. Irvin correctly explained that the common practice was to simply expend all ammunition once it was drawn from the facility. The lieutenant then suggested that we all go out on the firing line and detonate one mine each until they were gone. None of us really wanted to do that. Irvin came up with a very unusual counter proposal. I've already observed that this particular lieutenant was weak. He somehow lacked the moral authority required to lead soldiers in this type of unit.

Irvin's idea involved taking each of the mines out and using a K-bar knife to split the mine housings open. We would extract the C4 "plastic" explosive after dumping out the hundreds of ball bearings from each mine and combine all of it into one large explosive ball. He suggested that we could then take that ball out past the front of the range firing line and blow up one of the armored target hulks. This suggestion seems absurd now, but Irvin was very persuasive as he pointed out the relative training value for the use of these conventional mines in an unconventional way. The lieutenant finally agreed.

We proceeded to open up all nine of these mines and remove their contents without informing or consulting any of the troops waiting in the bleachers. When we had packed it all together, the thirteen and one half pounds of C4 explosive material was almost the size of a bowling ball. Irvin and the lieutenant gathered up the blasting caps, wire spools, and this huge ball of plastic destruction. They took the other sergeants from our platoon with them as they walked to the front of the firing line in a long single file. Irvin told me to stay at the ammo point with the medic as he was leaving, in case we had visitors.

We watched for quite a while as they walked out to one of the hulks about three hundred yards in front of the line. They looked like ants on a dead beetle as they worked on and around the target hulk placing C4, attaching blasting caps, and stringing the wire back to a central spot where it was all spliced together. They were in the process of moving slowly back toward us and pausing briefly to splice on more lengths of the electric wire. I looked around to observe the silhouettes of the troops in the bleachers and heard the noise of a jeep approaching the range from the main road on the other side of the hill.

I turned around just in time to see two radio antennae cresting the hill attached to the back of our company commander's jeep. Horrified, the medic and I turned toward Irvin and the lieutenant. There was nothing we could do to stop or warn them. As the jeep came to a stop, the company commander and first sergeant jumped out and looked around for someone in charge. Not seeing anyone else but me, the medic, and the crowd of troops in the bleachers, they both came walking briskly toward the ammunition disbursement point.

We stood inside the low wall with our toes against it at rigid attention. You never salute in the field. We were actually facing the firing line as the captain walked up and stopped right in front of me. I remember him asking "what is going on, Corporal Caringer?" I didn't respond immediately. I was slightly taller than the captain. I watched with morbid fascination as the leadership of my platoon stopped about halfway back from the target hulk to the firing line and began to get down into prone positions facing back toward the hulk.

The company commander was now staring at me with a troubled look on his face. I remember that he was wearing a very crisply starched fatigue uniform with his pistol belt and camouflage covered steel helmet looking almost new. I couldn't think of a more appropriate response to his question, so I just said, "I think we had better get down, sir!" The medic and I dropped down behind the low wall at the same time.

The largest explosion that I ever witnessed from within five hundred yards erupted about a half second later with ear shattering sound. Parts of the target hulk flew hundreds of feet in the air. A large section of steel actually dislodged from the rest of the vehicle and flew back toward the firing line. It seemed like it would narrowly miss one of the men lying out on the range. He saw it coming and dove out of the way. The smoke, dust, and debris flew so high and far from the source of the explosion that clods of dirt and small pieces of debris were falling on us all the way back at the ammunition disbursement point. I jumped to my feet as soon as it seemed to have stopped and resumed a position of rigid attention.

Glancing over at the bleachers, I noticed that they were now empty. I could see the silhouettes of arms, legs, and piled bodies on the ground under and behind them. The medic was standing next to me again as the captain slowly stood back up. The commander's face was brick red. As I recall, there was now a small clump of dirt and grass hanging from the front side of his steel helmet. The captain's uniform was now covered with dust and dirt.

He put his face very near mine and yelled, "I'm gonna..." That was all he could say. He spun away from me and took a few steps. Spinning back around, he stomped back over to me and stopped in the same place repeating "I'm gonna..." Walking away a few steps and then coming back again, he finally managed to ask me where my platoon leader and acting platoon sergeant were. At this moment, they were walking back toward the firing line again in a single file. They were laughing and knocking the dust and dirt off each other.

The captain realized what I was looking at and turned around to face them as they crossed the firing line. I believe they saw him at the same time because I noticed that Irvin immediately stopped laughing and tried to signal the lieutenant and the other sergeants to straighten up. The captain stomped down the hill and out onto the firing line where he intercepted the lieutenant and pulled him away from the others.

The first sergeant stepped over to me while this was happening and said something quietly about part of my anatomy now belonging to him. He was also a Vietnam veteran, and had severe burn scars all over his cheek and neck. He smoked cigars all the time. He apparently didn't like the idea of wasting any of them because he would smoke them until the butts were so short he almost needed a "roach-clip" to hold onto them. He was illegally smoking one at that moment in the immediate vicinity of our now empty ammunition control point. He pulled it out of his teeth with his thumb and forefinger and brushed a small piece of debris off his shoulder with the side of that same hand before blowing smoke in our faces and turning away to have a private conversation with Irvin.

I felt sorry for the lieutenant for the first time. I couldn't hear what was being said from that distance, but I could see that the captain was yelling into his face from about two inches away. I could see the lieutenant's head jerking backward with almost every syllable as if he was being struck physically. I don't remember much of what happened for the rest of that day. The platoon leader was relieved of his duties on the spot. The next time I saw him, he was working in division headquarters.

Irvin was a war hero. War heroes rated special treatment. He told me later that he had been given a formal letter of reprimand. As the ammunition disbursement point NCO, I could have been charged with criminal negligence in this incident. However, I believe most of the official fury was expended on the lieutenant. The army apparently figured that I was too junior to mess with. It took a long time for the rest of the troops in the company to fully get over this incident. We heard about it from all of them for months before the incident finally faded into almost legendary status and was painfully referred to from then on as the "Claymore Mine Range Incident".

I was sent to the Alcohol and Drug Abuse Coordinator's Course a short time later. Why I was selected to attend this course was a mystery to me. It may have simply been that my unit was required to fill a training slot and I was in the right place at the right time. This was a two week course covering the army's program for dealing with alcohol and drug abuse in the line units at Ft. Bragg. Successful completion of the course would label each graduate as a certified Alcohol and Drug Abuse (program) Coordinator. After completing the course, I returned to my company with this additional duty.

We now had a new, and more experienced, 1st lieutenant platoon leader. I believe my company commander and my new platoon leader were aware of my drug problem. It seemed very strange that they would place me in this extra duty position. It may be that they thought some of the counseling and training in the course would have a positive effect on me in some way. The program itself provided a small budget to be used for alcohol and drug abuse control purposes within each company size unit. I decided to make the best of it in my own covertly rebellious fashion.

I soon came up with a plan for using the ADAC funds to get a free trip to the beach. I put this together in writing and went to meet with my company commander in his office. The captain listened intently to me as I gave my presentation and seemed to actually agree with the plan. I knew what I was saying was complete hogwash as I was presenting it. I was trying to take advantage of the system. I couldn't have cared less about coordinating the alcohol and drug abuse program. My closest friends and I would have been the program's main targets if it had been executed correctly.

The plan I presented involved renting an entire hotel for a long weekend one block from the ocean at Myrtle Beach, SC. We would rent a full size tour bus from the Ft. Bragg Post Recreation Facility and take all of our company soldiers who lived in the barracks to the beach. There wasn't enough money in the fund to pay for this entire junket. However, each soldier would only have to spend about twenty dollars of their own money to make it possible.

The idea that I pitched was based on some fuzzy logic that I had invented in my head. I suggested that the reason why soldiers who lived in the barracks got involved in alcohol and drug abuse was because they were bored. There wasn't anything to do on post except go to the movies, swim at the pool, bowl, or hang out at the post NCO club and drink. This was not true of course, but it fit into the prevailing mindset of army leadership that regarded these average young soldiers as "barracks rats". The sale was made. To my amazement, the plan was authorized by the company commander as an actual project.

I took the next weekend and drove to Myrtle Beach with a friend of mine to look for a hotel. We found a small, but nice, hotel a block from the beach. I signed a binding contractual agreement with the hotel on behalf of my Army unit. My friend and I then spent the rest of that weekend partying and chasing girls on the beach. When we got back, I made the arrangements for the bus and got the "event" added to the unit training schedule. The company commander insisted that one of the junior lieutenants go with the bus as the Officer In Charge (OIC). I was to go as the Non-Commissioned Officer In Charge (NCOIC). We advertised this trip to all of the "barracks rats" and the group filled up very quickly.

I had been through the promotion board process just before this event. I received orders promoting me to the rank of sergeant E5 on the day we boarded the bus headed for the beach. As anyone reading this might imagine, this beach trip quickly devolved into one huge party that sickly resembled the drug and alcohol soaked debacles that the army was trying to stop in the first place. Large amounts of marijuana and other controlled substances were smuggled onto the bus. Alcohol was readily available, and a large number of available young women were discovered at Myrtle Beach that weekend. It turned out that there was a beach beauty contest being held at the same time.

The young lieutenant OIC was easily manipulated and the resulting chain of illegal events could have been pre-dicted. The fact that I was not prosecuted for some of the things that happened that weekend might possibly be attributed to the idea that my prosecution would have embarrassed the army somehow. Please don't misunderstand me on this. My behavior and attitude had sunk to a despicable level. I now believe my legal survival in these incidents was actually the result of God's grace and his future plans for my life.

I spent most of my waking hours, when not working, in a desperate search of unbridled hedonism. My pursuit of sex and drugs took all of my spare time and all the money I earned. I actually believed that the most important attribute I could achieve was to be considered "cool" by my alleged friends. No matter how hard I looked for satisfaction, I found myself broke, hung-over, and alone.

I read the story of the prodigal son now, and I can identify with him. The problem for me was that I couldn't just go home like he could. I was in the US Army. I knew God was and is real regardless of how I was living. I had been taught right from wrong. I misunderstood the real meaning of grace though. I believed I was lost and that there was no way I would ever be able to please God. During sober moments which I avoided diligently, I felt utterly hopeless. Even though I knew a lot of people that I called "friends", I was almost always desperately lonely.

I was in this mindset when I met my first wife. At our first encounter, I was walking through a city park on the far side of Fayetteville from Ft. Bragg on a sunny Sunday afternoon. My friends and I were always trying to pick up girls. We had developed the process into what, in our minds, approached an art form. This was just one more "opportunity" as I saw it. After striking up a conversation, I found that she was very friendly and we just seemed to click. We quickly agreed to spend some time getting to know each other. Within a few weeks, we were involved in an emotional and physical relationship that developed way too fast. In my desperate loneliness, I had begun to look for someone that I could settle down with. I had just turned twenty one years old. I irrationally felt like any chance I had for a regular life was quickly passing me by. As our relationship grew rapidly closer, I convinced myself that I needed to do something to change my circumstances and normalize my life.

I decided to ask this young woman to marry me without seeking wisdom or advice from God or my parents. If someone had questioned me at the time, I would have said that I desperately wanted a wife and family. I didn't understand then that what I desperately needed was the one relationship that could really fill my gnawing emptiness. I know now that this can only be satisfied by God the Father through His Son Jesus Christ. I didn't just fail to ask my parents for advice. I didn't even tell them anything about this decision until after it was made.

She said "yes" almost to my surprise. She was emancipated, but she was only seventeen years old. Her mother agreed to sign the required papers that would allow us to marry. It may seem cliché now, but there were many women in those days that lived near military bases seeking young soldiers who were lonely and gullible enough to get involved in ill advised marriages. These marriages were often short lived, but they produced children who were immediately considered army dependants. The mother of the children would be entitled to child support payments from the soldier whether the marriage lasted or not. The army would see to it that these payments were deducted from the soldier's pay as long as he remained in the service.

I'm not saying that my wife's intentions were mercenary like this, but I often wondered later if her mother thought that way. My new wife was unfortunately very similar to me in her lifestyle. We moved into a house off post owned by her parents, and our new marriage simply extended the party. I liked being married and I looked forward to coming home each evening.

I soon had to go to Alaska for a month to participate in arctic warfare training. My unit boarded C141 aircraft at Pope Air Force Base on October 23, 1978 wearing winter field uniforms designed for the type of winter climate found in the US mid Atlantic region. During the flight, we did what was called "in-flight rigging" of our parachutes and gear. We arrived many hours later over Ft. Wainright, Alaska after a very turbulent five thousand mile flight. The flight crew turned the air conditioning on to "full blast" mode to try and acclimatize us as much as possible to the expected air temperature we would encounter when we exited the aircraft.

Ft. Wainright seemed to be having a heat wave for the end of October in that region; the temperature on our arrival was about twenty degrees Fahrenheit. We didn't receive arctic weather gear until the day after we arrived by parachute. By the time we left Alaska thirty days later, the temperature was dipping down as low as fifty below zero. During this training operation, we learned to survive in extreme cold. We learned to use snow shoes, cross country skis, and Achio sleds. We spent a great deal of time out in the frozen tundra learning survival techniques. I lost about thirty pounds during the month and returned to North Carolina looking like animated skin and bones.

The most disturbing element of my return home was discovering that my new wife had been unfaithful to me with someone else in my absence. She had also managed to spend every dime of my payroll checks while I was gone. As you might imagine, I was furious and deeply hurt. A couple of weeks went by in which I struggled to control my reaction to what had happened.

I was at home on a Sunday afternoon in mid December watching my wife nonchalantly cooking something in the kitchen. I stepped over to her and gently reached around her to remove the utensil from her hand and guide her over to the carport door. Opening the door, I coaxed her outside without saying a word. It was a relatively warm afternoon full of bright late autumn sunlight. I stepped back into the house alone, quietly closed the door, and locked it leaving her out in the carport. She didn't knock on the door. I felt bad about what I had done after a few minutes. I stepped back over to the door and opened it to find that she was simply gone. I learned later that she had walked over to one of the neighbors' houses. She ended up moving back in with her parents while I tried to work and struggled with the mess my life had become.

Another couple of weeks went by and I found myself out in the woods on Ft. Bragg on another training exercise. It was the week before Christmas and I was very deeply depressed. I spoke with my section sergeant and he contacted the company commander who drove me back to garrison from the training exercise. He ordered me to report to the brigade chaplain for counseling. The chaplain was a Catholic major who had been an infantry officer in Vietnam.

After listening to most of my story, the chaplain told me that what I needed to do was to go out and make a large purchase for myself. This sounded like really weird advice, even to me. He insisted that it would help with my depression. He asked me if there was any large purchase that I would like to make but had hesitated to follow through on. I told him that we had considered buying a newer car. He said that was exactly what he wanted me to go and do. He also told my company to let me go home on leave for Christmas, even though I hadn't requested leave and didn't have enough accrued leave time. He then sent me home. No prayer was offered. No Biblical counseling was given.

I was absolutely at rock bottom emotionally when I got to the house. It wasn't just my messed up marriage. It was everything. My whole life was a sham. I had been playing both sides of the fence for so long that it was becoming difficult to keep everything straight anymore. I knew I was absolutely lost and separated from the life God wanted for me. I remember being in the house alone and dropping face first as I called out to God for mercy. I confessed my sin to Him. I asked Him to rescue me from myself and the mess I had made. I vowed to do whatever He wanted me to do if He would rescue me and put my family back together. I felt better after that and was able to sleep.

I decided to take the chaplain's advice the next day and went out to buy a new car. I ended up at the Toyota dealership on Bragg Boulevard and spent almost all day purchasing a brand new 1979 Toyota Corolla. My leave was scheduled to start at midnight. I intended to go home and sleep a few hours before signing out at the company orderly room and starting the drive to Missouri. On my way home, I saw my mother-in-law's car parked in front of a neighbor's house and realized that my wife was probably there visiting. I decided to stop and try to see her. I felt that I at least needed to let her know I was headed home on leave. When I talked to her, I was surprised to find that she was excited about the new car. I was really shocked when she asked if she could go to Missouri with me. I said yes. We made quick arrangements. In the middle of the night, we started the long drive together.

We were approaching Nashville, Tennessee on Interstate 40 at about 2:00PM the following day. We were getting along surprisingly well, but I was exhausted. There was part of a six pack of beer on the back floor of the car and a small bag of marijuana in the glove box. I had surrendered everything to Jesus the day before we left. She didn't even understand the concept of salvation. The marijuana and beer were hers. After the way I had been living, I didn't know how to start to explain to her that I would rather not have these things in the car.

I was pretty tired, and she offered to drive. I pulled over to the shoulder and we switched places. As she pulled the car back onto the interstate, I realized that this was the first time I had ridden in the passenger seat of this new vehicle. I began experimenting with the radio, the glove box, and the seat belt. This was the first car I had ever owned that had retracting shoulder belts.

Traffic was fairly heavy as we approached the city. She was driving in the left lane. She had the driver's side window down partly because it was a beautiful afternoon. I leaned forward in the passenger seat so that the shoulder strap extended all of the way out and said "look, this belt wouldn't stop me if we have a wreck…" She looked over at me and said "yes it would, it's supposed to do that".

I was looking down at the seat belt when I felt a violent jerk in the vehicle's movement. I looked up in time to see that she had let the left wheels move into the grass of the median strip. We were traveling at about 70mph. There was a drop-off of several inches where the concrete stopped and the grass started in the median. I was about to shout for her not to jerk the wheel to try to bring the car back onto the pavement, when she did exactly that. The left front tire bit into the edge of the concrete, and the car catapulted end over end. The next thing I knew, I was watching the windshield turn white and feeling the tumble as the car made about four complete flips and ended up on its roof.

I was hanging from the seat belt. The words that were ringing in my mind were "wow, I guess the seatbelt works…" Gasoline was pouring into the roof of the car from a gash that had been torn in the side of the tank. To my horror, I looked around and realized that my wife was no longer in the car. I undid the seatbelt and fell into the roof. I tried kicking the doors open and then realized that the driver's side window was gone.

I heard my wife screaming my name as I crawled out of the car from what seemed like far away. The wheels were still spinning on the car. I saw the gas filling the roof and lunged back into the car to turn off the ignition before a fire could start. I then looked around and saw that we had come to rest at the bottom of a deep ditch on the right side of the highway. My wife was sitting up about fifty yards down the ditch screaming in pain and panic.

I started running to her and noticed that a middle-aged lady was running down the embankment at the same time carrying a blanket. We reached her simultaneously, and the lady identified herself as a registered nurse. She told me not to try and move my wife and that help was on the way. I heard another vehicle skidding to a stop up on the road shoulder and looked up to see a fire truck with men spilling out to run down the embankment and lend assistance. The nurse and the firemen had been in just the right place to witness the accident without getting caught up in it.

The firemen kept the car from burning and had an ambulance headed to the scene within minutes. In what seemed like a very short time, the EMTs were carefully loading my wife onto a rigid stretcher board and carrying her up to the ambulance. As they were putting her into the back of the vehicle, I <u>felt</u> God say, "This is what you asked Me for." It was astounding. It was also very clear to me. I climbed into the back of the ambulance with her and we were on our way to the hospital.

The car was taken to a local salvage yard for storage and disposition. In the emergency room, we learned that my wife had a broken shoulder blade and a severe laceration on her lower back. She would be held over night and released the next day for convalescence at home unless other injuries were found. I called my parents and told them what had happened. They agreed to drive down to Nashville and pick us up at the hospital when she was released.

Christmas was good that year. Because of this accident, I got to stay home an extra week on emergency leave. My new wife met my parents for the first time. We decided that it was best for her to stay there with them for an extra month while I went back to Ft. Bragg. During extensive conversations with my dad, she also made a profession of faith in Christ Jesus. The insurance company replaced the car with another brand new one after I paid the deductible. I was a completely different person when I returned to my unit at Ft. Bragg than the one who had left a few weeks earlier. It was now January 1979. I was due to finish my active duty service in May that year. I had a new lease on life and had made a firm commitment to completely change my lifestyle. I still didn't fully understand God's awesome grace and the free gift of salvation.

Chapter 8

Subdued Sinner

"The LORD is good,
a stronghold in the day of trouble;
He knows those who take refuge in Him."
(Nahum 1:7)

I made no secret of my new commitment to Christ when I returned to Ft. Bragg. Many of my friends, at first, treated me like it was a passing phase I was going through. Some of them simply laughed at me. Some of them treated me with open contempt. I didn't really care. For the first time in as long as I could remember, I really felt redeemed. I refused to return to the moral cesspool I had escaped from. I believed then, and still believe now, that I had heard or felt the voice of God. I saw hope for a future that didn't include failure and dependence on drugs and alcohol. It was much more than turning over a new leaf for me. I had made a commitment that I intended to keep.

I immediately stopped using the drugs I had been so heavily involved with for so long. I stopped drinking at the same time. I believed that if I completely changed my lifestyle, I would be honoring the promise I had made to God. My whole train of reasoning was caught up in the idea that God had saved me through His grace, but I had to deliver on my vow to change and do as I had said "whatever He wanted me to do".

I didn't comprehend it then, but this was just an extension of the same religious reasoning that I had engaged in all my life to that point. I didn't understand that there are a great many religions in the world. All of them are constructed around a philosophy that requires man to do or not do something in order to be accepted by the religious object of worship. I didn't understand that true Christianity is not based on anything we can do. It is based on what Jesus did for us. Real Christianity involves absolute surrender to Christ the King to be sure. This is only made possible by the redemptive sacrifice Jesus gave on the cross of Calvary. This was the highest price ever paid for anything or anyone, and it was paid for us while we were all hopelessly lost sinners.

The Holy Spirit draws us to Jesus. Jesus says in John 14:6, "I am the Way, and the Truth, and the Life. No one comes to the Father except through Me." Jesus lived a perfect life for about 33 years before freely giving Himself on the cross. The punishment He took there was my punishment. The death that He died was the death I deserved for my rebellion against God. He did it for me personally. He personally gave His life for every descendent of Adam and Eve, although very few people will accept His awesome gift. He died in our place so that

He could trade us His perfection for our corruption. He declared "It is finished" as He gave up His life and died. He didn't stay dead. He conquered death. Three days later, He rose from the tomb and took His rightful place as The King.

All we have to do is accept His sacrifice and surrender our corrupt lives to Him. That surrender brings about a new relationship with God through His grace. Real Christianity is the acceptance of a free gift. All true gifts are free of cost or they are not truly gifts. They are either accepted or not, but they can't be earned. To try to pay for a gift would be an absurd insult to the giver. We are called to repent or turn away from our old life to a life governed by the King of Kings. We are saved for good works not by good works. In his letter to the church at Ephesus, the apostle Paul explained, "By grace you have been saved through faith. And this is not your own doing; it is the gift of God, not a result of works, so that no one may boast. For, we are His workmanship, created in Christ Jesus for good works, which God prepared beforehand that we should walk in them."

The most significant misunderstanding for me was in regard to God's love and our promised adoption into His family. I was now on a mission to change my life. I didn't understand. All I needed to do was believe Him, surrender, accept this most magnificent of all Gifts, relax in the grace of God, and let Him change me. Instead, I tried to change myself in my own strength. I didn't understand that God's grace is immeasurably more powerful than our weakness and propensity for failure. The results were as predictable as they were disastrous.

I quickly became a social pariah to most of the other men in my platoon. I had been enmeshed in some serious illegal activities with the other sergeants in the platoon for over a year at this point. I was immediately mistrusted when I showed up touting my new life. Some of the men that I thought were my closest friends now refused to have anything to do with me. Some began to openly ridicule me and my beliefs. God blessed my work, on the other hand, and my performance as a soldier and leader improved greatly. Some might argue that the absence of drugs and alcohol had to positively impact my performance. I would readily agree. However, there was clearly more to it than that. I gained favor in several situations where the only explanation I could find was God's intervention. I was reading and studying the Bible, but I was not going to church and I was not being discipled by mature believers. I did feel God's grace on my work and it showed up in some amazing ways.

Our company was rapidly approaching the moment when it would have to pass its first ARTEP evaluation as a new unit in order to be certified as combat ready. The training regimen was intensifying. My section sergeant left the army at this time. I was moved into his duty position which was one pay grade higher than my own. We promoted one of the more mature specialists in the section to the rank of corporal. He took over my old duties as squad leader.

This meant that I was now responsible for myself and seven other soldiers. The section's equipment included two TOW missile launchers, four jeeps, multiple radio systems, two trailers, and a great deal of other miscellaneous gear. On any combat mission, I would be responsible for the care, deployment, and tactical use of as many as 70 TOW Missiles. My section would be attached to an infantry company or battalion adding a very powerful anti- armor capability to the unit commander's arsenal. The destructive potential of this many TOW missiles if they were properly employed would have to be considered militarily priceless. They could have made a very significant tactical impact on almost any battlefield situation.

We had trained so intensely by this time that we were beginning to develop our own tactical theories and methods. This was a pretty heavy responsibility for a 21 year old sergeant. I don't remember having any misgivings. I believed that I would perform my duties correctly if the need arose. This confidence was developed through relentless repetitive training. I also had the Holy Spirit of God helping and strengthening me. My wife returned to North Carolina at the end of January. The difficult events that had occurred at the end of the year were put behind us by choice.

My company was sent to Ft. Bliss, Texas in February to train in the high desert at a place called McGregor Range. This was a two week exercise that involved extensive maneuvers with an armored unit from Ft. Riley, Kansas acting as aggressors for us. It was quite cold the whole time we were there. The arid rolling hills and scarce vegetation of this high desert terrain made it very similar to several countries in the Middle-East.

My section was encamped at the military crest of a small hill early one morning overlooking a dirt road that was considered a main supply route. Our mission was to watch over the road and provide anti-armor protection for the company headquarters Tactical Operation Center (TOC) which was located in a small gully just behind our hill and about fifty yards away. The TOC in this instance was made up of a large army tent and a place to park a couple of jeeps. There was a canvas lister bag hanging from a tripod about ten yards from the tent with ice and fresh water in it for the headquarters staff. The headquarters staff normally consisted of the company commander, the company executive officer, the first sergeant, the operations sergeant, the supply sergeant, the armorer, and a few privates. The only people at the TOC on this particular morning were the operations sergeant and one of the privates.

I feel compelled to point out that there was no love lost between the company headquarters enlisted personnel and the members of the company TOW sections. I suppose this was completely natural because the headquarters personnel were always perceived as getting the best chow and a warm dry place to sleep. My men and I had been living out in the open for several days. It gets very cold in the high desert at night in February. We had been eating C-rations and drinking the rubber tasting water from our supply cans and canteens. As I listened to my men talking that morning, it became clear that they were starting to complain about this perceived inequality. They had started referring to the enlisted members of the company headquarters in several very derogatory ways. As the gray light of dawn slowly intensified, one of my gunners asked me if they could "bomb" the TOC. I knew what he meant, but I initially considered it a really bad idea.

It was not uncommon to discover alternative uses for things during the many long hours we spent in the field with the equipment we were issued. One of our discoveries involved the TOW missile launch tube trainer. The launch tube trainer was externally shaped like an actual missile launch tube. The inside of it was filled with some type of ceramic or concrete that made it weigh the same as a standard missile load even though it was functionally empty. The center of this tube was hollow. There were two electric terminal posts near the back end of this hollow space. A very small electrically triggered explosive device was connected to the terminal posts and pushed into the hollow center during launch training. The explosive would detonate sending out a loud report and a bright flash when the launch button on the traversing unit was depressed. This was intended to simulate the back-blast created during an actual missile launch. It was supposed to add necessary realism to gunner training.

I'm not exactly sure how we discovered this, but a C-ration can of beef and potatoes was just the right diameter to fit into the hole in the back of the launch tube trainer. We would put a couple of the explosive charges into the tube first and then insert the C-ration can on top of them. Turning the launcher around backwards and pointing the front of it toward the ground at an angle, you could aim the back of the tube skyward in the direction of an intended target and press the launch button. The resultant explosion would send a full can of beef and potatoes as far as fifty to seventy five yards depending on the terrain and the number of simulation charges it had been loaded with. I was the one who drew the C-ration meal which included beef and potatoes in the ration draw that morning.

We were discussing the possibility of actually dropping my chow can close to the TOC tent when the operations sergeant came out of the tent and walked toward the lister bag with an empty canteen. I reasoned that the potential morale boost for my men outweighed the relatively slight danger of actually hitting anybody with a C-ration can fired from that distance. I agreed to supervise the attempt, in a snap decision, as long as we used all of the missile launch commands adapted for this unique training opportunity. I produced the ammunition. My crew quickly loaded my canned breakfast on top of two explosive charges.

We methodically stepped through all of the target acquisition and prelaunch commands as we lined up the shot like the professionals we were supposed to be. The launch command was followed by a loud concussive boom. My can of beef and potatoes went streaking through the sky toward the space between the tent and the lister bag. The operations sergeant had finished filling his canteen and was walking back toward the tent. The projectile struck the ground in front of him and ricocheted up to strike him in the back of his right calf knocking his legs out from under him. He must have heard faint cheering from the hilltop because he shook his fist at us as he got back up and went to find what had hit him. He disappeared into the tent after picking up the damaged can.

We heard a jeep coming up the road from beyond the TOC at that moment. I realized that it was being driven by the company executive officer. The XO was a good lieutenant. I thought a moment and realized that the best way to head off any problems from the operations sergeant's expected complaint to the XO was to go down and face the music immediately. I told my men to return to their duties under the supervision of the corporal and started down the hill at a brisk walk. I arrived at the tent, opened the flap, and stepped inside. The lieutenant was sitting at a field table doing some paperwork. The private was asleep on a cot. The operations sergeant was sitting on another cot rubbing his calf. He looked like he may have been crying. The scene was strangely similar to what I had observed in my elementary school principal's outer office after I had thrown a rock at the school bully in the sixth grade. I tried not to hesitate as I said, "Excuse me sir, has anybody seen my breakfast?" The lieutenant looked up with a stifled grin and said, "You mean this?" He reached down and placed the dented C-ration can on the table in front of him. I said, "Yes sir! That's it!" He tossed me the can and said something like, "be careful what you're shooting at." I said, "Yes sir!" and walked back up to my position to finish breakfast.

Each of the nine TOW sections in the company would be given the opportunity to fire one live TOW missile near the end of this training exercise. This was a very rare event. Almost all of our launch training was done using computer simulators because live missiles were extremely expensive. Our company commander announced that he intended to turn this event into a competition between the TOW sections. He would score the performance of each section and announce the winning section when the exercise was complete. The prize to the winner would be an extra day off for the whole section when we returned to Ft. Bragg. My men performed very well and won the competition outright. We soon flew back to North Carolina. It was great to have the extra day off, but this didn't do anything to endear me to my fellow section leaders.

The primary mission of any real airborne unit is battlefield interdiction. The airborne capability of parachute forces allows them to be dropped behind the battlefront in enemy rear areas. These troops act as tremendous force multipliers for the commander of friendly forces as they force enemy commanders to deal with powerful light infantry elements actively disrupting their interior communication and supply lines. This is the reason airborne forces were developed in the first place during the early days of WWII.

A great deal of our preparation for potential combat operations involved familiarization on various weapon systems with this potential primary mission in mind. It also included training on escape and evasion. Ft. Bragg has many elaborate training facilities. One of these was a mock POW camp with all of the expected barbed wire, guard towers, cruel guards, and other "training aids". Our company went through an escape and evasion exercise during the weeks after our return from Ft. Bliss. We were delivered to Holland Drop Zone on the far end of Ft. Bragg one section at a time. We were required to escape from there and evade capture as we made our way across the largest training areas on post to a safe extraction point about twenty miles away. There would be many "aggressors" hunting for us. We would be taken to the POW camp, if we were caught, for intense training on resistance and continued efforts to escape. The exercise was to cover a 36 hour period, as I recall. We would be home free and the exercise would be complete if we made it to the extraction point successfully without being captured. That's the way it was explained to us at least.

We were trucked out to the DZ in sections and dropped at the side of the wood line. This type of operation is done in two man teams. I broke my men up into pairs as soon as we were dropped and the trucks disappeared. I sent them off with the best instructions I could give them; "This is where you're headed, don't get caught". The newest private in my section was a very thin young black man named Cooper. I decided to keep him with me. I told Cooper to follow me and do what I told him without question as soon as the rest of the troops had faded into the woods. I had already made up my mind that there was no way I was going to allow myself or my teammate to get captured. I checked out the area and found that there were no aggressors anywhere near us. I then began moving quickly along the edge of the drop zone headed directly south and then west away from the extraction point.

I reasoned that the aggressors had information regarding our most direct route of escape. The last thing I wanted to do was anything that would strengthen their intelligence advantage. I planned to do the unexpected. Some rigidly pedantic leg infantry officers might think of this as "cheating". The concept of "cheating" did not apply and was not even possible in this scenario the way I looked at it. Our objective was to escape. We were taught that we were to train as we would fight because we would fight like we had trained. I would never have willingly allowed either of us to attempt evasive travel along a predictable route if Cooper and I had been in an actual combat situation.

We continued heading straight west as we cleared the southwest corner of the drop zone. We eventually crossed the Ft. Bragg perimeter and moved into civilian terrain near Kings Highway. We must have been a strange sight for anyone able to see us as we moved up near the shoulder of the highway in full camouflage wearing steel helmets, carrying rucksacks, and M-16 rifles. I had probably broken several laws by leaving Ft. Bragg in this manner, but training was training. The highway was more or less deserted. I hadn't really worked out yet how we would reenter Ft. Bragg at a point where we could approach the extraction point from a more advantageous direction.

We suddenly saw a car approaching from the south. I decided to take a huge chance and flag down this vehicle. I would give them some type of story that was forming vaguely in the back of my head. We could easily move back through the woods away from the highway and the danger if the occupants turned out to be any kind of threat. They would have an impossible task trying to tell who we were. We didn't have anything on us that would identify either of us. It's not likely anyone could pick us out of a line-up the way we were camouflaged. We were both painted several shades of woodland green. I motioned Cooper to stay where he was and stepped out onto the shoulder motioning the vehicle to pull over and stop. I saw that it was occupied by three young men in civilian clothes with very short military style haircuts.

I moved up to the passenger window and asked who they were. They identified themselves as US Marines from Camp Lejeune, North Carolina. They were at Ft. Bragg on temporary duty (TDY) orders for training. All three of them were staring at me like I had just landed on the front lawn of the White House from an alien space ship. I decided then and there to simply tell my nautical infantry cousins the truth and ask them for a lift back onto Ft. Bragg. They were a little shocked, but they immediately realized what we were doing and agreed to help us if they could. I motioned Cooper up onto the road shoulder and we piled into the vehicle. I explained a good route onto post that would keep all of us out of trouble.

We were soon headed to the 82nd Airborne "Old Division Area" between Pope AFB and Longstreet Road. I'm not saying this was a favorite spot, but it was interestingly close to the location of an earlier bonfire incident. The marines may have agreed with army leg infantry officers who would have judged our actions as cheating. However, they also saw that what we were doing made pragmatic sense. They thought it was very funny in any case. I believe they had a great laugh with our help. I asked them to drop us off near a remote Post Exchange snack bar location. We went inside and spent the rest of the day playing pin-ball and trying to look as inconspicuous as possible to the few personnel who occasionally came in and out. This would have been a daunting task for two heavily armed green men anywhere else, but this was Ft. Bragg. There were always strange things to see in this place.

Afternoon progressed toward evening and I told Cooper it was time to go. We hoisted our equipment and headed back out toward the training area from a totally unexpected direction. It was several miles to the planned extraction point. It was still a lot closer than our original starting point at Holland Drop Zone had been. I found a hill that provided an excellent view of our objective from a direction perpendicular to the expected route of approach when we finally neared the extraction point. We camped there for the night and took turns keeping watch. We watched for a while as vehicles came and went from the extraction point when dawn came.

We saw successful teams of "escapees" reach the extraction point periodically. They were marshaled in a growing group out in front of the lone building at the location. I told Cooper it was time to go when the exercise time limit came near, and we sprinted down the hill to the objective. We registered our successful escape with the company operations personnel at the front of the building. Our weapons were taken by the armorer. We were then told to ground our gear and join the still growing crowd of troops in the front yard.

The exercise time limit elapsed as we sat in the yard. We were all expecting to be trucked back to the barracks, so we were not surprised when 2½ ton trucks pulled into the driveway and senior sergeants started ordering everyone aboard. We realized that we were not, in fact, headed back to garrison as the trucks pulled out of the drive. Loud inquiry was soon rewarded with stunning information. The company commander had decided that the aggressors had failed to capture enough of us to fully utilize the mock POW camp during the exercise. He had also decided that the training value to be gained from sending all of us to the POW camp (whether we had successfully escaped or not) couldn't be passed up.

It seemed like the old saying, "What goes around comes around", was in full play here. It didn't occur to me at the time that one of the people involved in these training activities may have been the same operations sergeant I had "shared" my breakfast with at Ft. Bliss one morning in February. This kind of "shady deal" didn't do anything to make the TOW sections feel any better about the company headquarters personnel. It seemed to us that there really was some "cheating" involved in this particular Escape and Evasion exercise.

Time passed very quickly as we prepared to go through the ARTEP evaluation tests. My wife and I weren't involved in a church. We continued to read the Bible and try to live out what we were reading. Our company was preparing to undergo one of the most important milestone tests for a new unit in the US Army. It turned out to be a lot more difficult and complicated than most of the unit leaders expected when the testing finally arrived. The army worked very hard to make these evaluation exercises as realistic as possible. When it was all over, my section was the only section in the company that had passed. The company as a whole failed. Several weeks went by while our unit was still not certified "combat ready" as a unit. If we had to be deployed for any real world contingency, the company would be cut up and parceled out to the three infantry battalions in the brigade as "strap hangers" and reinforcements.

The training cycle ended and our brigade entered the six-week DRB1 Mission Cycle. In the early part of the mission cycle, each unit went through several practice alerts and Emergency Deployment Readiness Exercises (EDRE). Some of these EDREs involved assembling and preparing to move to the debarkation point at Pope Air Force Base's "Green Ramp". Many of them only involved telephonic practice alerts used to make sure the men living off post could be reached if necessary in the time required.

Our unit had gone through its share of practice alerts as Easter weekend of 1979 neared. We were getting close to the end of the mission cycle. I thought I had the system figured out. I really wanted to get away from Ft. Bragg for the four day Easter weekend. The time remaining in my enlistment was growing very short. My Elapsed Time in Service (ETS) date was rapidly approaching. My company commander, first sergeant, and platoon leader were beginning to apply pressure to try and get me to reenlist. I had no intention of doing that. I was really looking forward to getting out and going home.

We had been married about five months. I had not yet been able to take my wife on any kind of honeymoon trip. I had all of this going through my head when I made a very stupid decision that could easily have landed me in jail. I decided to take my new wife to Disney World in Orlando, Florida over the Easter weekend. The problem was that I was not supposed to be more than two hours away from Ft. Bragg during this portion of the DRB1 Mission Cycle. I reasoned and rationalized with the facts competing against my selfish desires and a growingly prideful attitude. It was strangely similar to the imma-ture thought process I used as a child when I decided to tear up a note from my elementary school principal. We had been through all of the practice alerts we were likely to go through. The cycle was almost over. The only alert we would have during the holiday weekend would be a telephonic one, unless some real world emergency happened.

I stupidly decided to take the chance. I may have begun to feel somewhat invincible since I had gotten away with so much illegal activity over the years. I had broken so many rules, that one more chancy scheme didn't seem to matter. What I was not considering was that I was now a professing Christian. My new wife and I were living with her parents and her younger siblings at their large house in Fayetteville. I called the sergeant whose name was ahead of mine on the telephonic list. I asked him to skip me on the list and call my corporal directly during any practice alert. I called the corporal and told him to call the next name on the list if he got a call from the sergeant above me. We packed up our new Toyota and headed south to Florida that Friday morning. On Saturday, we had a great day at Disneyworld.

We returned to the hotel exhausted. I decided to turn on the TV in our room and watch the news as my wife was taking a shower. I found a network news broadcast and saw a still image on the screen of an old bearded man wearing a turban. I turned up the volume just in time to hear the newscaster explain that this was the Ayatollah Khomeini. He went on to say that this Ayatollah person was somehow responsible for the fall of the Shah of Iran. I listened in terrified fascination. The newscaster nonchalantly announced that the president had decided to alert the 82nd Airborne Division for possible deployment to Iran. The paratroopers would be sent to ensure the safe evacuation of American civilians from this now former ally. Reality came slamming into my thought process. I was soon shouting for my wife to dry herself, get dressed, and get to the car. I grabbed our belongings in any way I could pick them up and threw them into the trunk.

My wife realized that this was not a drill and quickly worked herself into the spirit of our dilemma. We were soon driving up the freeway as fast as that Toyota Corolla could travel. We amazingly made it back to Fayetteville in almost record time without getting stopped by the highway patrol units of four different states. We finally made it home, and my young sister-in-law came out to tell me how much trouble I was in. She said that men from my company had called, and they seemed really mad.

I ran into the house and immediately called the company. I recognized the first sergeant's voice as he answered the phone after only one or two rings. I told him who I was and he thanked me very kindly for condescending to bother calling in during this national emergency. He then barked something like "You had better get here right now, specialist...!" Since I was a sergeant, not a specialist, it dawned on me that in the first sergeant's opinion, I was likely to lose at least one pay-grade through this event. I dressed as quickly as possible and ran out with my alert bag.

The barracks was nearly deserted when I got there. The only people I could find were the Armorer, the first sergeant, and all of the company commissioned officers including the commander and my platoon Leader. The officers and the first sergeant were all sitting in his office playing cards. I stood in the doorway for what seemed like ages while they quietly finished the hand. The officers then got up and walked out of the room without saying much of anything. The first sergeant looked up at me and quietly asked me to come inside and close the door. He then delivered one of the most artistic chewings I had received to date in my military career. At the end of it, he told me that I was very fortunate that the unit had not yet actually deployed. The first sergeant explained that all of the sections had been broken down and distributed through the brigade as fillers and reinforcements. I was to draw my weapon and protective mask from the arms room and go wait in my platoon area until further instructions were given.

The deployment was soon cancelled as things turned out. The US Marines were used to evacuate the largest group of American and NATO civilians from Iran. This development changed the potential charges against me from desertion to simply being absent without leave or AWOL. I was not the only soldier in the company that had failed their duty in this incident, but I was the most senior. The company armorer (a corporal) and about ten privates had also been AWOL.

We were all given non-judicial punishment under Article 15 of the Uniform Code of Military Justice (UCMJ). I stood at rigid attention in front of my company commander's desk as he explained the charges against me, the foolishness of my actions, and the punishment he was giving me. I was fined $150 dollars and given two weeks extra duty. The other miscreants were given the same punishment. As noncommissioned officers, the armorer and I were put in charge of the extra duty cleaning detail which involved two hours cleaning company facilities every night for two weeks.

The first sergeant came into the orderly room on a Sunday afternoon near the end of this justifiably humiliating extra duty tour. He ordered me and the armorer to follow him into the latrine. I assumed he was going to point out some problem with the cleaning process. The first sergeant turned to us as we entered the latrine and informed us that if we ever told anyone what he was about to do, he would personally kill both of us. He then reached into his shirt and pulled out the original and file copies of our Article 15 paperwork. He handed these documents to us and told us that we would still lose the money portion of the punishment, but that he didn't want the written portion to show up on our permanent military records. They were, after all, still trying to get me to reenlist. I didn't see this for what it really was. God was again protecting me and my future even in my foolishness.

The army began releasing me from duties and responsibilities over the next few weeks. I began the clearing process as I prepared to separate from active duty. I signed out of the Company for the last time on May 8th, the day before my 22nd birthday. My wife and I headed home to Missouri on what was known as "terminal leave". We celebrated my birthday at my parent's home. I began the process of searching for a civilian job. One adventure had ended. Life had some strange turns in store for me yet.

Chapter 9

Lonely Reprobate

"For God so loved the world, that He gave His Only Son,
that whoever believes in Him should not perish,
but have eternal life."
(John 3:16)

We lived with my parents for a few weeks while I tried to find a job. I was finally hired by a fraternal benefit society as an insurance salesman. We soon had our own apartment and I was really beginning to enjoy being a civilian. We soon learned that we were expecting a child. I was ecstatic. Selling insurance was one of the most boring things I had done in a long time, but life as a whole was really improving in my opinion. We got involved in the church that my sister attended. We began to grow a little more in our walk with God. It seemed like we were both adapting well to the civilian world at first. The months passed quickly until my first daughter was born on June 11, 1980. I couldn't believe how good life had become.

The overwhelming joy of being present when my daughter was born was astounding and difficult to explain. She was delivered at a small clinic in Mt. Vernon, Missouri. The clinic rules allowed me to stay in the room with her throughout her first night. The bonding was complete. This tiny beautiful creature had stolen her father's heart. We named her Catherine Anne. I spent as much time as I could with my wife and our new daughter for the next several months. We took the baby to church and dedicated her to God as soon as possible. I was working hard to make a living for my family and still trying to spend as much time as possible at home as the end of the year drew near. I didn't realize, at first, that serious problems were developing in my relationship with my wife. By the time I did understand, it was too late.

My wife told me at the end of the first week of December that she wanted to take the baby and go back to North Carolina to spend Christmas with her folks. I couldn't get the time off to make this trip right away. She suggested that she would go ahead on the bus. I could drive out to join them at her parent's home on Christmas Eve. We would spend Christmas with her family and drive home together the following day. I really didn't want to be separated at that time, but I didn't want to be selfish either.

I put my wife and baby daughter on a bus headed to North Carolina on or about December 10th with a very heavy heart. The next two weeks passed so slowly it was almost unbearable. I was finally able to make the drive and arrived as planned on Christmas Eve. We had a happy reunion and a warm holiday celebration that lasted right up to Christmas afternoon. I told my wife that I thought we needed to get our things together and get on the road headed home when the celebration ended. The atmosphere immediately changed in our guest room. She looked at me with a strangely cold expression and told me that she was not going back with me. I was shocked and silent at first. I soon became angry when I realized she wasn't kidding. I angrily told her that was fine with me. I would get the baby's things together and be on my way with her as soon as possible. She told me that I wouldn't be allowed to leave the house with our child. She had decided that my religious pursuit was too much for her. She wanted to return to the old party life-style before she got any older.

I was in shock and I didn't know how to respond. I opened the guestroom door and moved out into the hallway seeking air. I walked past the bedroom door of my wife's younger step brother and saw that he was sitting on his bed with a shotgun in his hands. There was an overwhelming sense of malevolent purpose in the house. I returned to our room to try and reason with my wife. She made it clear to me that she was completely resolved in her decision. I wasn't welcome to stay. There was nothing I could do to safely take my daughter with me. This plan had apparently been developed with the assistance of my mother-in-law. I was out in the car slamming my fist into the dash board in grief driven rage before I could fully grasp what was happening. I drove back home in a fog of sadness, anger, and crushed dreams over the next twenty hours or so. My parents were almost as shocked as I was when I told them what had happened.

I tried to keep moving on with life, but everything seemed like it had stopped working at once. I changed jobs a few times over the next couple of months and reenlisted in the army reserve at the same time. I wanted to stay busy to keep my mind occupied. My parents later told me that they believed I had gone through some kind of emotional breakdown. I don't doubt it. I struggled with growing frustration and anger while at the same time trying to hold on to what I thought was my Christian faith.

A real understanding of God's grace and love would have had a tremendous impact on my decision making in this period of my life. I read and prayed. I went to church and tried to share my beliefs with others. I felt like I was being called into vocational ministry. However, I couldn't square this up with the disaster that my life had become again. My parents were very supportive and continued to try to encourage me in every way. I was still trying to survive in my own strength. With every successive failure I sank deeper into depression and despair.

The army reserve unit I joined was the 1st Battalion of the 12th Special Forces Group. I was given an operations sergeant position in battalion headquarters working for the Battalion S3 Operations Officer. I stayed with this unit making monthly drills until I finished my initial six year commitment to the army.

I had moved in with my sister Susan and her young daughter Bethany. Our parents owned the house where we lived in Springfield, Missouri. Dad had changed his denominational affiliation from the Nazarene Church to the Assemblies of God. He was now serving as the pastor of the First Assembly of God Church in Buffalo, Missouri. Susan was struggling to make a living while starting college as a single mom. Neither of us made much money. Even though we didn't have to pay rent, we barely managed to keep the lights on and have food in the house.

I desperately needed grace, but I didn't understand that God's grace was there all along. Even though I was still legally married, I started dating. I was looking for someone to fill the lonely void I felt. I realize now that I desperately wanted to be respected, but I felt like such a foolish loser. I swiftly lost most of my self respect and confidence. I made up for this by being dishonest, boastful, and arrogant. I tried to continue showing a cheerfully religious façade to those around me while I became ever darker on the inside.

I eventually finished my commitment and was discharged from the army reserve. I learned from my father that one of his former parishioners had moved to Oklahoma to take part in the oil boom that was happening there. Dad suggested that this family friend would give me a place to stay so that I could get a fresh start if I wanted to get away from Missouri. I thought about it for a short time and jumped on the opportunity. I now owned an old four-door Chrysler sedan that I had purchased from my uncle. It didn't take long to pile all of my earthly possessions into this huge boat of a car. I headed toward Woodward, Oklahoma where I hoped to find some way of filling the void that my life had become.

I arrived in Woodward in June of 1981. This small town is located in northwest Oklahoma very near the "panhandle" portion of the state. The 1980 census had shown a population of about thirteen thousand. The oil boom had swelled this number exponentially by the time I arrived. Staying with dad's friend and his family allowed me to diligently seek employment. I had a vague idea that I wanted to work in the oil fields. I also had a growing interest in law enforcement.

All the time I had spent on the wrong side of the law combined with my selective but religiously pedantic view of right and wrong to make law enforcement seem very appealing. In my understanding of police organizations, they appeared to have a distinctly military atmosphere about them. I missed the regimentation of the Army even though I really didn't understand why. I had applied earlier for employment with the Missouri Highway Patrol, but was turned down because my vision wasn't good enough to pass the physical. As I turned in applications to several oil drilling and oil well service companies, I also decided to apply for employment with the Woodward Police Department.

I managed to land a job working as a floor hand for an oil well service company within a few days. My first day on this job was my last. We spent fifteen hours that day, in excruciating heat, trying over and over again to cut a piece of pipe deep in the well. This involved sending knife after knife down into the pipe to score it at a certain point. We then lifted the pipe to a great height and released it. We let it fall to an abrupt stop over and over again trying to get it to snap where it had been scored. This went on all day. I would have stayed on this job even though it was one of the hardest workdays I had experienced for quite some time, but another opportunity overtook this one immediately.

I was pleased to learn that another job offer was waiting for me when I finally got back to my friend's house that night. The Assistant Chief of Police had come by the house to try and recruit me while I had been out on the rig that day. He left a message that he would like to see me in his office as soon as possible. I made it a point to be standing in front of him the very next morning. I don't remember any of the interview process that I went through before I was hired. I somehow passed the physical this time.

I was employed as a patrolman. This was the Woodward Police Department equivalent to the army rank of private. I was issued uniforms and equipment and started work almost immediately riding with a senior patrolman on the day shift while I waited to enter the Oklahoma Basic Police Academy. The department figured they could use the extra manpower to help with simple tasks under the supervision of experienced officers. The training and experience new officers received in this way were quite valuable as they prepared to attend the police academy.

The population of this town had virtually exploded as the oil business boomed. Young men were moving in from all over the country. In some cases they were coming from all over the world. There was a growing shortage of housing. There wasn't enough city street capacity to handle all the traffic. There was a tremendous influx of cash along with people trying to spend it. There was also a predictable increase in criminal activity. I was happy to be involved in something that was as challenging as it was distracting during the summer of 1981. The population had more than tripled by 1982. I made friends quickly with many of the officers in the department. I also accepted a part time job catching shoplifters at a local grocery store. I met a beautiful young lady while working in the evenings at this extra job and quickly became way too involved with her.

I was separated from my wife through no choice of my own, but we were still legally married. I was desperately searching for companionship and was once again driven by my flesh rather than God's Word and His plan for my life. I had made a promise never to return to the use of illicit drugs, but I had once again started abusing alcohol. I was drinking when I wasn't working. I believed the alcohol was helping me cope with the pain I was swimming in. It certainly deadened my recognition and awareness of right and wrong.

I spent about a month riding along with senior police officers and trying to learn as much as I could through observation. I finally reported to the police academy and began earning my state certification as a police officer. The Oklahoma Basic Police Academy is operated by the Oklahoma Council of Law Enforcement Education and Training. The state now has a campus used for this purpose in Oklahoma City.

The Academy was held on the grounds of the Marlan Estate in Ponca City in 1981. The Marlan Estate consists of a large piece of land with a beautiful mansion designed to resemble a French villa. The Estate was built in the 1920s by former Oklahoma Governor Marlan. Governor Marlan was also the founder of Conoco Oil Company. The estate once had its own private lake, a formidable stone wall, and several surrounding buildings including gate houses and guest houses. The mansion itself was a marvel of engineering in its time. It even had its share of secret passages and things that would have made it a fascinating place to live. The Estate ended up belonging to the Catholic Church for a time and was used as a convent after the deaths of Governor Marlan and his heirs. The lake was drained and the huge swimming pool was filled in. The church erected an additional dormitory building near the mansion to house the nuns. I have no idea how they made use of the mansion itself.

The estate eventually became the property of the State of Oklahoma. The state built a convention center on one side of the property. The mansion had fallen into tragic disrepair, but the state finally recognized it for what it was and began restoring it as a museum and priceless historic landmark. The Council of Law Enforcement Education and Training was allowed to use the dormitory for housing police academy cadets. They used the convention center kitchens as a mess hall of sorts, and academy classes were held in the various gate houses. Firearms training was held at the local firing range owned and operated by the Ponca City Police Department.

Basic police academy was shorter than army basic training, but there was a lot more information packed into it. Many of our classes were taught by instructors from the state, but several classes were taught by a special agent from the FBI. The training was very intense, very comprehensive, and very realistic. After passing the evaluation exams at the end of the process, we became police officers certified by the State of Oklahoma and we were on our way back to our various jurisdictions.

I was assigned to work on the evening (4:00PM to Midnight) shift when I returned to Woodward. We didn't rotate shifts as some departments do. Once an officer was assigned to a shift, they stayed on that shift unless they were promoted or left the department for one reason or another. I stayed on the evening patrol shift at the Woodward Police Department for the next four years.

I had asked my new girlfriend to marry me as soon as I was able to finalize my divorce. She agreed. We drove back to Missouri after I graduated from the academy, and began the legal process to end my first marriage. Again, I hadn't sought God's will or guidance in these very important decisions. I was bull-headed in my determination to do what I wanted to do even though I knew deep in my heart that what I was doing was foolish and wrong.

My wife called the house from North Carolina and wanted to talk with me while we were in Springfield, Missouri during this trip. It seemed that she had had a change of heart and now wanted to return to the marriage. This was one of those salient moments when I could have done the Godly thing. I should have recognized that she had reached her own "end of self" moment. I should have forgiven her and reconciled our broken relationship. I foolishly told her no and hung the phone up on her in a stubborn flash of anger and vendetta fueled with confusion and doubt. This one choice not to forgive, this one failure to act in true Biblical love and grace, subsequently caused great damage and pain for many people in the years to come. So many things could have been different had I not acted in pride and selfishness in this one critical moment of decision. Life changing choices are often like that. This is why God's grace is so immeasurably important.

I entered another ill advised marriage a month later. I realized this was a tragic mistake almost immediately. My new wife and I didn't get along from the very beginning. There were constant money problems. We disagreed on almost every imaginable subject. The disagreements soon turned to anger and mistrust. There was no grace and no peace in our home. My mindset was so warped at this point, that it was easy for me to be unfaithful to this marriage both emotionally and physically. A nearly constant cycle of hostility ending in fights punctuated by apologies and imagined peace followed up by more hostility ending in fights started almost immediately. This lasted through the rest of our seventeen year relationship.

My son Gregory was born on June 17, 1982, almost exactly nine months after the start of my second marriage. I bonded quickly with Gregory as I had with my daughter Cathy Anne. However, my past emotional baggage and my prideful selfishness were compounded with the difficult relationship I had with Gregory's mother. This kept me from being the kind of father he needed. I never did get it right.

I gradually developed into a professional law enforcement officer at work, at least on the surface. I managed to somehow cover up my immoral and illegal behavior off the job while showing a propensity for performance on the job in much the same way I had handled my early days in the army. The evening shift for patrol officers in this very busy little town was often quite intense. We experienced long periods of extreme boredom punctuated by brief encounters with stark terror like police officers almost everywhere.

The working lives of police men and women in this town and other small towns in Oklahoma, Texas, and Kansas were a little different during the oil boom because of the rapid population growth and the dramatic influx of easy money. We encountered criminal activities ranging from narcotics trafficking to armed robbery, burglary, rape, murder, and all kinds of other crimes too numerous to list.

These things seemed strangely out of place in this small community. The situation reminded me of stories I had read about the sudden development of towns and cities in old California during the mid nineteenth century gold rush. This once sleepy little town suddenly had to deal with virtually all kinds of criminal activities that would normally be expected only in much larger metropolitan areas on either coast. This criminal activity was overlaid with an increased occurrence of domestic disturbances, bar fights, traffic accidents, and countless other police concerns. The increased population didn't simply increase the activity in proportion to the growth. It multiplied the activity beyond our ability to understand or cope. Some of the things we encountered were humorous, but most of them were frightening and deeply disturbing.

The day shift officers usually had an easy life. They dealt with traffic problems and more administrative law enforcement matters most of the time. The evening shift tended to be the busiest shift. It encompassed the time period when "good people" were winding down and going home to do "good people" things. "Bad people" were starting to come out into the public to do their "bad people" things. It seemed like most of the bad things occurred while these two disparate groups of people were awake and active at the same time. The officers working the midnight to 8:00AM shift had their own special circumstances to wrestle with. The sheer volume of activity on the evening shift created a strain on everyone involved. This strain would potentially have affected any sane person with a gradual erosion of patience and self control. So many things happened during this period, that it would be very difficult, if not impossible, to describe them all.

I was assigned to guard a crime scene for several hours late one night not long after my graduation from police academy. The incident that happened at this scene was the bludgeoning murder of a young man. The detectives were still working the scene. They left it the way it was found until they could return during daylight. The body had been removed. This was my first exposure to protecting evidence at the scene of a violent crime. I knew things like this happened often, but this was the first time I had been this close to it personally. It was a graphic reminder of the depravity of man. It was also a very lonely post to stand on that long dark night.

I participated in sorting out a great many public and private disturbances. These were often domestic fights of one kind of another. There were also a great many bar fights and brawls. It was not unusual to get in a physical fight during a shift, especially during the weekends. I had a ride along passenger one night in the person of one of the local businessmen. I stopped a car for speeding only to find out that it was occupied by two drunken brothers who would always fight with each other if a policeman wasn't available. I happened to be available that night. I got behind them and turned on the red and blue lights. They turned off the main street onto a smaller two lane side street and stopped. The passenger in the suspect vehicle stayed in the car at first as the driver got out to walk back toward me. I realized that he smelled like he had been bathing in alcohol and he was unstable on his feet. I asked him to walk a straight line, and he was unable to do so. His speech was slurred. It was obvious that he was intoxicated.

I asked him to put his hands on the trunk lid of his car and quickly frisked him to ensure he wasn't armed. I reached around him, grasped his left wrist, and pulled it behind his back. I managed to get one side of my handcuffs onto that wrist and was holding his left arm behind him, while I reached for his right wrist. The passenger came out of his side of the vehicle at that moment and stormed around the car in a screaming rage. He demanded to know what I was doing to his brother. The fight was on. I moved back to the passenger side of my patrol car using the body of the first brother as a shield to blunt his sibling's attack. My ride-along guest looked terrified but had the presence of mind to hand me the radio microphone through the open window. The dispatcher already knew my location because the stop had been called in before I got out of the car. I was only able to shout something about needing assistance before I had to focus all of my attention on the problem at hand.

There was no doubt in my mind during this incident. My life was threatened. Fighting two drunken maniacs at the same time is not easy even if you have a strong grip on a handcuff that is holding one subject's arm behind his back. I was using my feet, my flashlight, and the body of one of the men to fight off his brother as I recall. They were biting, kicking, punching, and screaming all at the same time. I will admit that I briefly considered simply shooting one of the brothers in self defense and then beating the other one into submission with my flashlight. Reason thankfully prevailed. I heard sirens coming from several different directions within seconds after my radio call. Help arrived in a few minutes, but it seemed like much longer. We were finally able to bring both men under control. This kind of violent event was sadly not at all unusual.

I was called on another occasion to assist an officer who had stopped a suspicious van near the downtown area. The back doors of the van swung open as the officer had approached the vehicle on foot from his patrol car. One of the occupants of the vehicle aimed a sawed off shotgun at the policeman. The driver of the van hit the accelerator before shots could be exchanged and the vehicle sped off down the street. The officer ran back to his car and gave chase while calling for support from other patrol vehicles. There was a phalanx of about eight patrol cars chasing this van down the highway within a few minutes. The vehicle was forced to stop by a highway patrolman nearly ramming it head on. We all came to a stop and jumped out of our vehicles to approach the van from protective angles. The suspects opened the side door of the van and scrambled out trying to escape across a field next to the roadway. It's an amazing miracle that none of the four men in this vehicle were shot in this incident. They were all apprehended without any physical harm to them or the officers involved. It turned out that they had been casing the downtown area planning to burglarize one of the local businesses.

I was on patrol late one night when I answered a radio call describing an injury accident just outside the city limits on a dirt road near an intersection. An ambulance was being dispatched, but they believed their response time would be too long to help in this situation. The dispatcher acknowledged my location when I gave it. She told me to respond because I was the nearest emergency unit to the accident scene. I saw a small older car on its side near the road shoulder as I approached the scene. A man was on his back in the road about 15 yards in front of the car. There was a house near the road junction, and several people were standing on the front porch looking out at the wreck. It was obvious what had happened. The car had been driving up the dirt road very fast and the driver had lost control when he encountered a series of washed out ruts running across the road surface. The vehicle had veered over to the left and slammed into a dirt mound before turning onto its side.

The driver was the only person in the vehicle. He had not been wearing a seat belt. His body had slammed against the steering wheel when the car struck the dirt mound. He had climbed out of the vehicle and managed to walk to where I found him before collapsing on the road. The people in the house had witnessed the accident from the porch and had called 911. They had not come out to offer first aid or assistance. The driver was still alive when I got to him. His chest and lower face were crushed. Huge bubbles of mucous and blood were growing out of what was left of his mouth as he fought to breathe. I had been given extensive first aid training in both the military and police academy. I knew that I needed to clear his airway. I simply couldn't figure out how to do that in this case. There wasn't enough to work with. His lower face was smashed. Everything below his upper teeth was smashed into a bloody mass of broken bone, torn skin, and blood. His eyes were staring up at me as I crouched over him trying to figure out how to save him. I watched the life go out of him in desperate frustration and sadness. He simply died in my arms and there was nothing I could do to stop it. Chemical testing later showed that he was extremely intoxicated when the accident happened. The ambulance crew told me not to worry about it, that there was nothing I could have done. I would like to believe that, but it seems likely that there must have been something.

I was working a double shift one night covering for a friend of mine who was assigned to the midnight shift. I was on normal patrol during the very early morning hours when the dispatcher announced that there had been an injury producing accident that involved fire at a busy intersection on the south side of town. Available units were requested to assist the primary unit and the fire department with traffic and crowd control. I responded and took a position blocking the highway on one side of the accident scene. The tragedy involved a single older model pickup truck that had flipped onto its side and caught fire as the fuel escaped from a torn open gas tank and ignited to incinerate two of the cabin occupants.

There had been three people in the truck. They had been racing with another vehicle just before the accident occurred. The investigation revealed that the two vehicles had come in contact with each other as they drove around a sweeping turn. This had caused the truck to flip onto its driver side. The driver of the pickup, a young woman, was killed instantly. The man sitting on the passenger side of the truck managed to struggle out of the passenger window by standing on the other occupants even though the truck was immediately engulfed in an explosion and flame. The third occupant, another young woman, was caught in the middle of the cabin and tried to escape by climbing up and out through the same passenger window.

My very good friend and shift leader, Lieutenant Les Morton, reached the scene right after the first explosion. He leapt onto the side of the truck when he heard the woman screaming in the flames. Les heroically reached into the cab through the open window and grabbed the woman by her hands to try to lift her out. A secondary explosion suddenly blew him backward off the truck and the woman sank back to her death. These things had just happened when I arrived. The male victim was sitting on the ground next to the truck screaming in agony as the skin from his hands and arms literally fell away due to severe third degree burns. Les was furious that he had failed to save the woman. He immediately became very quiet and covered up the trauma with deliberate professional calm. I stood in the highway blocking traffic from my end of the accident scene. The smoke from the burning truck and the roasting bodies blew directly into my face for what seemed like an eternity. The fire department finally put the fire out and removed the bodies for transport to the mortuary. The lone survivor was taken to the hospital and the debris was removed from the highway.

I was later sent to deliver the blood alcohol kits to the mortuary. Les supervised the protection of the evidence as the Coroner extracted a large vile of blood from the driver's body. The chemical test revealed that the driver had a blood alcohol content that was well above the legal limit. We all went back on patrol and continued through the rest of the shift as though nothing unusual had occurred. It was cold the night this happened. I was wearing a regulation fur collared uniform jacket as I stood in the smoke of this senseless tragedy. I never could get the smell of smoke out of that jacket. I eventually just threw the jacket away, but I found it much more difficult to discard the memory of that dense black smoke.

I had taken my wife to a movie one night while trying to enjoy some off duty time. An argument started on the way home from the theater over something totally inconsequential. This was sadly not unusual. We reached our apartment and I started to unlock the front door. We could hear the phone ringing on the inside. Cell phones as we know them now didn't yet exist. The police dispatchers had been trying to reach me, but they didn't know where I was. I rushed into the apartment and answered the phone. One of the dispatchers began talking to me in a terribly strained voice as though she was reading from some kind of script. She said, "We need you immediately. We have shots fired and officers down in an incident at…" She went on to give the location and told me that all department officers were being called out to participate in an extensive manhunt. The incident had occurred less than thirty minutes earlier. I was to report to the chief of police at a particular location to receive further instructions. I didn't bother trying to explain what was going on to my wife. I went out, got on my personal motorcycle, and rode as quickly as I could to the location as instructed.

I learned when I arrived that the incident involved a drug bust that had gone terribly wrong. Our Detective Division had been working with members of the Oklahoma Bureau of Narcotics to bring about the arrest of a known distributor of methamphetamine. The OBN officer supervising the operation was a young captain who happened to be a personal friend of the Oklahoma governor. He was in an unmarked van with one of his sergeants, one of our detective sergeants, and a female informant or "snitch". Our detective sergeant in this vehicle was a good friend of mine named Mark Chumley.

They had made arrangements to meet the suspect and his girlfriend in a restaurant parking lot to make a drug buy. The operation was loosely cordoned by several of our detectives in unmarked vehicles along with other members of the Bureau of Narcotics. The captain was driving the unmarked van, and the snitch was sitting in the passenger seat. The two sergeants were sitting in the back. There were no windows in the back of the van, so no one could see these two men from the outside. They drove into the parking lot when the time came and saw the suspect vehicle parked at the very front corner near the sidewalk. There was a small car parked right next to it and an empty parking space on the other side of that. Much of the rest of the lot was full. The captain pulled the van into the empty parking space without thinking it through apparently.

The snitch got out and walked around to the suspect vehicle. She got into the car and a sharp conversation took place between her and the male and female suspects. The snitch got back out of the car a few minutes later and walked around to the passenger side door of the van. She climbed in and told the officers that the male suspect was in the driver's seat and his girlfriend was in the passenger seat. She told them there was a sawed off pump shotgun lying on the back floor of the car in a spot where it could be easily grabbed by the driver. She had made the deal and purchased an amount of methamphetamine for $1300 cash. She produced the bag of drugs and dropped it between the seats.

The captain seized this moment without warning anyone on his team. He abruptly climbed out of the driver door of the van. The suspect vehicle was still sitting where it had been. The suspects may have been counting the money or discussing something, but they had not yet backed their vehicle out. The captain walked briskly around the small car parked next to the suspect vehicle and approached the open passenger side window where the female suspect was seated. This all happened so quickly that the two sergeants hadn't yet managed to exit the passenger side rear door of the van. The captain ridiculously opened his badge case as he approached the window and shouted "State Police, you are under arrest!" Those were his last words. The suspect moved the shotgun up and fired it past his girlfriend's face directly into the captain's chest. He died instantly.

Sergeant Chumley and the Bureau of Narcotics sergeant were out of the van now. Chumley heard the shotgun blast as he moved to a spot behind the van where he would have a better vantage point but no protective cover. The OBN sergeant went under the van and came up on the other side of the separating vehicle. The suspect had climbed out of his driver's door and moved quickly to the left rear side of his car immediately after firing the first fatal shot. Chumley saw the mangled body of the captain that was now draped over the roof of the car next to the suspect vehicle. He immediately began firing round after round into the suspect vehicle until his service revolver was empty. The suspect lunged up from the left rear quarter of his car when Chumley stopped firing, and shot him directly in the face from about thirty feet away.

The OBN sergeant couldn't see what was happening as he came up from behind the intervening vehicle. He fired his pistol into the suspect vehicle over the body of his now dead captain until the weapon was empty. He then ducked back down and quickly started to reload. Chumley was still alive and lay in the middle of the parking lot screaming. The suspect ran right past him without shooting him again and disappeared into a darkened housing area next to the restaurant parking lot.

The female suspect had been hit several times through the car door, but she was also still alive. She had somehow managed to climb out through the driver's side door of her vehicle. She was crawling across the street in front of the restaurant trailing blood and torn body parts when the cordon officers made it to the scene a few seconds later. All of the restaurant patrons were now on the floor of the restaurant in terror. One officer was dead, another officer and one suspect were severely wounded, and the other suspect was gone. The entire gun battle had lasted less than thirty seconds.

A very large number of police personnel were already on the scene when I arrived. Over one hundred officers from throughout the county responded to the call for assistance. A tight cordon was quickly established around the entire area. Those of us not involved in the cordon were partnered into teams of three officers each and sent into the dark alleys of the housing area to try and find the suspect or flush him out into the open. I was teamed up with our department's day shift Patrol Lieutenant and an Auxiliary Sheriff's Deputy.

It's very difficult to describe the anxiety we all felt as we began to slowly search this dark foreboding area looking for an armed suspect that had already shot two police officers. We moved into the darkness as quietly as possible with labored breath and our hearts pounding. None of us dared use any kind of light because it would provide warning of our approach and an easy target. Every dog bark or twig snap as we moved through the back yards and alleys was almost enough to undo us. The suspect finally heard the search heading his way and buried the shotgun behind a garden shed. He then walked out onto a side street with his hands on his head. He was apprehended without further resistance by one of the officers on the outer cordon.

The Bureau of Narcotics captain was buried with honors in a ceremony presided over by the Oklahoma Governor. Mark Chumley survived the shotgun blast that he took in the face because he was far enough away from the shooter. The shot pattern was wide spread. All of the pellets missed his eyes, and none of them penetrated deeply enough to strike his brain. He looked like he had serious acne from the pellet scars after he got out of the hospital months later. He returned to duty as a detective within the year.

The female suspect also survived. She was tried and convicted as an accessory to this heinous crime after numerous surgeries which were paid for by the people of Oklahoma. The male suspect never expressed any remorse for his actions. He was later heard bragging to news reporters on the courthouse steps that he was glad he had done it and would do it again if he had the chance. The State of Oklahoma decided not to allow him that chance. They eventually gave him a lethal injection at the McAllister State Penitentiary after all of his appeals were denied. The rest of us learned that the training we had been given regarding the proper approach to a suspect vehicle could have saved this young captain's life, if he had followed it.

I was patrolling in the downtown area late one night when I observed a young man walking up the sidewalk on the opposite side of the street carrying a strange container that appeared to be heavy. There was something weird about the way he was walking and what he was carrying. I decided to find out more. I made a U-turn and called for assistance with this pedestrian contact. I pulled the patrol car over to the side of the street and stopped. I got out and left the driver door open as I stepped forward and asked the man to stop. He turned toward me and, I saw that the container was actually a plastic soap dispenser reservoir that you might find in a public restroom. It was filled with coins.

I asked for some identification from the young man, and he put the container on the hood of my car while he dug into his pockets. I was thinking that he may have burglarized a service station or something as I tried to find an explanation for a commercial soap dispenser full of loose change. The young man handed me a folded piece of paper as my backup officer arrived and parked behind my vehicle. The other officer walked up from behind and to my left as I unfolded it. The piece of paper turned out to be a birth certificate. It was the only identification he had.

I stepped back to my car and called in the man's name and birth date with a coded request to have the information checked for wants or warrants. I had stepped back around the door toward the young man when the dispatcher called back saying that there was a warrant hit on the subject. This was also in code, but the young man was looking right at me and must have seen a change in my expression. He snatched up the container of coins and heaved it at my backup officer, striking him in the chest and almost knocking him down. He then spun around and took off running like a frightened gazelle.

I shouted instructions to my backup and ran after the subject. He ran down the sidewalk to a side street and turned right. He reached the opening of the alley that ran behind the building fronting the main street and turned left down the alley. The alley literally went down hill steeply here. There was a board fence that came away from the corner of the building and ran along the edge of the alley out toward the sidewalk. Several old tires and some pallets were stacked against the fence. I didn't realize that the alley dropped down hill behind this fence.

I thought I could catch the fleeing man if I cut through the side lot and jumped over the fence. There wasn't a great deal of light in this area. I went up over the old tires at a dead run and vaulted over the fence with little understanding of what I would find on the other side.

The ground, to my horror, was not where I thought it would be. I found myself falling through the darkness. I landed on the fleeing subject and we both slammed into the ground. The fight was brief and painful. I had dislocated my right shoulder when I landed. The only real advantage I had was that I had stunned him when I landed on top of him. I discovered that he had a long hunting knife in a sheath at the small of his back while I wrestled with him trying to force one of his arms behind his back. I ripped the knife away with my left hand and threw it as far as I could. I had finally managed to get the subject onto his face with his wrist behind him, and my knee in his back, when my backup officer came sliding around the corner in his patrol car and nearly ran over both of us. He managed to bring the vehicle to a stop with the bumper just inches from my already injured shoulder. We never did figure out where the soap dispenser and loose change had come from. The young man proved to be a runaway juvenile. He was turned over to Child Protective Services. I worked light duty for the next six weeks with my right arm taped to my chest.

Not everything that happened was dangerous or tragic. Some of the things we experienced were genuinely funny and some of them were just strange. There was a strong camaraderie that developed between most of the officers I worked with. We practiced ambulance humor as a means of dealing with many of the tragedies we witnessed, and we pulled more practical jokes on each other than we probably should have.

We had a running contest for "one-upmanship" with the fire department crew that occupied the central fire station sleeping quarters when they were not out on a fire call. The central fire station was located perpendicular to the police department. Their upper windows overlooked our patrol car parking lot. The firemen often collected buckets of snowballs during the winter and stored them for use against unsuspecting police officers as they came and went from this parking lot. The firemen would rain snowballs on the otherwise defenseless officers when they thought they could get away with it from the tactical advantage of their much greater altitude.

My shift lieutenant called all of the patrolmen on our shift to the city parking lot one night about a block away from the police department. He told us that he had had enough with the snowballs from the firemen. Leaving someone on patrol in case of real emergencies, he told the rest of us to prepare as many snowballs as we could carry. He then led us in a long single file line in a manner that reminded me of the infantry patrolling I had learned earlier through the intervening parking lots, yards, and bushes to a rear door of the fire department. He had somehow managed to obtain a key to this door. Once it was open, we had completely unfettered access to the enemy's domicile.

We crept up the back stairs and discovered one of their five gallon buckets of snowballs near one of the hated window ledges. It was clear that they felt very secure in their evil lair because they were all fast asleep. We changed that within seconds. Liberal amounts of snow were applied to our sleeping antagonists in an extremely satisfactory manner. The only drawback was that one of our fellow officers was slightly injured when he chased one of the firemen down the vertical pole slide into the truck bay and rammed his leg into something when he lost his footing on the now wet concrete floor. The Chief of Police somehow heard about this incident later and we got yelled at. The firemen never again used the upper windows of their sleeping quarters to launch projectiles at us while we were trying to do our jobs.

Our department did not have separate divisions for patrol and traffic control. All of the uniformed officers were responsible for both activities. I didn't personally concentrate much effort toward traffic control. I usually wouldn't make a traffic stop unless the driver was exceeding the speed limit by at least eleven miles per hour or appeared to be doing something else that would clearly endanger themselves or others. I did carefully watch for any evidence of people driving while intoxicated or impaired. I had investigated or assisted with several fatal traffic accidents in a relatively short time. All of these and most of the serious injury accidents I had worked involved alcohol in one way or another. It was clear to me that this was a critically important part of traffic law enforcement because of the harm caused by chemically impaired drivers. I didn't write a great many traffic tickets, but I made a lot of DUI arrests with this understanding.

There were always a lot of traffic accidents to contend with anyway. The number of drivers trying to make use of the limited road network in this boom town seemed to make these mishaps inevitable. I investigated or assisted other officers with thirteen separate traffic accidents on one particularly busy Tuesday evening shift. One of the accidents that night involved a pickup truck and a train. This was a warm Tuesday night. It wasn't raining. There was no fog. No other inclement conditions existed. It seemed like everyone who was due for a car crash decided to go out and get it over with that evening.

We had snow on top of freezing rain one afternoon during a particularly cold winter. The roads were so slick a pedestrian could barely stand up on them. The city had been advertising through the local news media all day begging people to simply stay home and not try to drive anywhere. They were asked to exchange driver information and insurance cards if they were involved in an accident unless injuries or fatalities were involved. They were told to get the vehicles removed from the roadways in any way possible. We had limited our patrolling that day to what was absolutely necessary. I received a call that to go to a particular intersection near one of the city parks that afternoon. I was to assist with an accident that had apparently turned into a disturbance of some kind. I approached the accident scene very slowly and had a few minutes to observe what was going on from a distance. The accident involved a customized van and a pickup truck at a "T" intersection. The van had apparently run into the back of the pickup as it was stopped at the stop sign. The parties were not fighting; contrary to the report we had been given. They were working diligently together to get the vehicle bumpers unlocked from each other so that they could go on about their business.

I continued to slowly approach the scene from slightly up hill and behind the van. I was about a hundred and fifty yards away when I saw that they had finally managed to disengage the two vehicles from each other. I was traveling at about ten miles per hour and I decided to slow almost to a walk as I approached the scene. I immediately found that there was nothing I could do to slow down. The brakes were useless. I even tried putting the car in reverse and spinning the wheels backward. Nothing worked. I tried driving up onto the ice covered curb. It didn't help. I wasn't sure I could make it around the vehicles either. I did slow down a little, but I was traveling at four or five miles per hour when I realized that a collision was unavoidable.

The people were still celebrating over their success in separating the van and truck. I got on the public address system and warned them to get away from the vehicles because I couldn't stop. I had finally slowed down to walk speed and gently tapped into the rear bumper of the van. This knocked it back into the pickup truck and again locked the bumpers together. One can only imagine my embarrassment and the insults I received from the people I had been sent to help.

A report has to be made any time a police car is involved in an accident. I called my lieutenant over the radio and told him what had happened. He said he was on his way. I soon saw him slowly approaching from the other street. He turned up the street we were on just as the people were again freeing the vehicle bumpers from each other. He had plenty of time to take note of the entire scene. He rolled his window down and approached my vehicle very slowly as if he was going to stop in the street and speak with me. I rolled my window down to get the lecture I knew I deserved. He didn't stop. His car rolled past mine at a slow walk pace while he stared at me with a disgusted look on his face. I distinctly heard him very quietly say, "Caringer, you are an idiot…" The fact that I agreed with him didn't do anything to help my self esteem. He just kept going. I never heard anything else about it as far as I can remember.

I was enjoying some precious time off one very stormy summer afternoon when I got a phone call from one of the sergeants in the detective division. He told me that there had been a brutal murder the previous night at a two story apartment house in an older subdivision. A young single mother, who acted as the property manager, was living in the bottom apartment with her baby. Two young adult brothers occupied the upper apartment. Someone had viciously murdered the young woman during the previous night. The murderer had doused the body with gasoline and set the building on fire after laying the baby on the ground outside the front window. The fire had obviously been an attempt to destroy available evidence. One of the two brothers had been detained as a material witness. The other young man was missing. The detectives had several reasons for believing that the missing brother had committed the crime. They had been working the scene all day, but they had not yet finished collecting evidence. The suspect was still at large.

The detective explained that they didn't have enough patrolmen available to guard the scene over night while they continued the search for the missing man. He asked if I would be interested in overtime pay for guarding the scene. I told him I wasn't interested. He almost started begging. He solemnly promised me that I would only have to watch the scene for a couple of hours until they found a replacement for me. I finally agreed. He told me to change into a regular duty uniform and pick up a patrol car at the police department. He gave me the address and told me to meet him there as soon as possible because he couldn't leave the scene until I arrived.

The detectives had packed up all of their gear and were ready to leave for the evening by the time I got there. They planned to return first thing in the morning. I was escorted around the perimeter of the crime scene while it was still daylight and shown where everything had happened. It was important to know these details because critical evidence was still potentially scattered all over the area. The house was an older two story building with an exterior stairway that allowed access to the upper floor without entry to the lower floor. The house was still standing, but it had been severely damaged in the fire. The windows were gone from the lower floor and the front door was standing open. Smoke and water damage made details hard to see on the inside of the lower floor as the daylight faded.

I parked the patrol car across the driveway at the entry from the street. The detectives again promised me I would be relieved in two hours and then drove away. The thunder storms that had been threatening all afternoon arrived soon after. I periodically got out of the car and patrolled around the house perimeter in the rain. I tried to effectively guard the scene as I waited for relief. The two hours passed pretty quickly and no relief arrived. The evening shift lieutenant came by, after another thirty minutes, and brought me some coffee. This was my regular supervisor. I asked him about my relief and he told me that he had nothing to do with it because he was short handed and this was a detective division operation.

Another hour went by and the storm was now furious. The rain was coming down in sheets and the wind was blowing fiercely. Thunder was crashing and lightening was striking all around me. I got out of the car and made another quick patrol around the crime scene. Nothing was visible unless I saw it in the beam of my flashlight or the brief brilliant flashes of lightening. I climbed back into the car to get out of the rain. I turned on the FM radio to ease the boredom. I scanned through the channels and came to a radio theater presentation. I've always liked Radio Theater. This happened to be one of the old programs like "Lights Out" or "Suspense". I remember that this presentation was very intense. The program came to the place where the story was about to reach its dramatic conclusion. The tense background music was building up. I was getting into it. My nerves were on end. There was a sudden bright flash of lightening and a tremendous crash of thunder. It was almost as if these were part of the radio program. A large white object flew out of the front window of the house at that same moment. I was looking straight ahead when this happened, and I only saw it in my peripheral vision. The screaming that I heard then was my own. I got out and went to see what had happened after I managed to peel myself off of the vehicle headliner.

It turned out that the "white" object was a large Persian cat that had decided to leave the house through the open window at just the right moment. I went back to the car and called the dispatcher on the radio. I told her to call the detective in charge of the case at his home and let him know I was leaving the scene within the next hour whether he had found me some relief or not. I think everyone listening on the radio understood I was serious. My relief arrived about thirty minutes later.

My home life was very troubled. My wife and I rarely agreed about anything. My life at work was intense and often violent. I tragically tended to bring the stress and tension home with me rather than leaving it behind on the job. I hear stories about soldiers returning from combat with post traumatic stress disorder and now recognize a lot of the symptoms. It's clear to me now that many of the difficult behavioral issues I displayed during this time in my life were compounded by the nature of my employment. I also understand that I wasn't seeking help from Jesus Christ, the only real source of relief. My wife and I got along like gasoline and matches. The number of domestic disturbances at my own home continued to grow in intensity and anger.

Chapter 10

Aging Rebel

"As a father shows compassion to his children,
so the LORD shows compassion to those who fear Him.
For He knows our frame;
He remembers that we are dust."
(Psalm 103:13-14)

My first wife was given custody of my oldest daughter in our divorce. The distance between Oklahoma and North Carolina made visitation very difficult. My daughter was with me for short periods through her first few years. This was very hard for both of us. My marriage was almost always in turmoil. This ensured that my daughter was treated like a step child whenever she was in my home. I was given custody of her in a consent agreement when she was four years old. I sent her to North Carolina about a year later for a short scheduled visit. Her mother disappeared with her and I did not know where she was for the next three years.

I quickly got to the place where I desperately wanted to be anywhere else but home. I decided to go to college and pursue a bachelor's degree in Law Enforcement. I learned that the Veterans Administration would pay me a regular monthly income check as part of the GI Bill if I enrolled in college and maintained a full study schedule. I promptly enrolled at Northwest Oklahoma State University for the spring semester in January of 1983. I was able to go to school a few mornings each week while continuing to work on the evening shift at the police department. I still worked several hours per week catching shoplifters at the grocery store whenever possible.

It was at this time that I began to miss life in the army and decided to join the Oklahoma National Guard. I soon found myself with one more additional job working in the fire direction control track in B Battery of the 1st Battalion, 189th Field Artillery. My duties in the National Guard involved a weekend drill once per month and a two week training camp each summer. I hadn't been in the National Guard very long before I decided to also join the ROTC program at Northwestern and add army officer training to my list of weekly activities. I was sleeping very little by the middle of the year in 1983 and spending almost all of my time away from home.

I barely graduated from high school as a teen because my study habits were so bad and my grades were abysmal. I really didn't know what to expect when I started college at age 26. I wanted to go to college, unlike high school, and I soon found that this made all of the difference in the world. I was interested in most of the subjects and my study habits were necessarily much more diligent. I made the dean's list and president's list in the first two semesters. I struggled with a few classes later but somehow managed to finish well and ended up graduating with a 3.5 grade point average. I found that most of the classes when I got involved in the ROTC program covered subjects that I was very familiar with from my prior military service. I also had a strong interest in the classes that were not as familiar to me.

I realized during the final semester of ROTC that Army bureaucratic logic would determine my future occupational specialty as an officer based on what branch of the Army I was working in for the National Guard at the time I was commissioned. I didn't want to be commissioned as a field artillery officer. I was a working police officer and I was going to obtain a degree in Law Enforcement. I decided to transfer to a military police unit within the Oklahoma National Guard. I made this transfer while I was still in school and worked for a short time as a platoon leader in the 745th Military Police Company.

I went to school straight through for three years beginning in January of 1983 and finishing with all of the credits needed to obtain a Bachelor of Science degree in December of 1985. I had majored in law enforcement and minored in sociology and military science. My youngest daughter, Jennifer, was born in the spring of 1985. My academic and military training grades were surprisingly high when I finished the ROTC program. I was given the Distinguished Military Graduate Award from the university and offered a regular army commission as a military police 2nd lieutenant by the US government. Most ROTC graduates entered the army as reserve officers on active duty. Regular army commissions were given to service academy graduates and ROTC distinguished military graduates. This was a great honor. I talked with my wife about it, but I didn't consult God.

I accepted the regular army commission and received orders to report to Ft. McClellan, Alabama in January of 1986 for the Military Police Officer Basic Course. I was back in the army on active duty. My professional life looked very promising. My personal life was a wreck. My relationship with God could not have been seen on any list of personal priorities. My marriage was a shambles. My finances were abysmal. My pride insisted that my peers see me as a solid, decisive, and intelligent young professional. I was too stupid, however, to realize how miserably inept I was regarding things that really matter. We were deeply in debt and I couldn't see any way to pay what we owed. We sought legal help and ended up filing for bankruptcy protection while I was in training at Ft. McClellan. I can't imagine what my army superiors must have thought about this new regular army 2nd lieutenant starting his career in personal bankruptcy.

God's amazing grace was evident even in this. I attended the army conventional physical security school at Ft. McClellan immediately following the 17 weeks of officer basic course. I was assigned after that to the 295th MP Company at Seneca Army Depot, NY. We lost our personal vehicle and most of our larger possessions in the bankruptcy. The army flew us to upstate New York, and we were picked up at the airport by an army van that took us to the temporary housing available at Seneca. Seneca Army Depot no longer exists. It became a victim of the Base Closure Act several years ago after the demise of the Soviet Union. This was a very important storage and maintenance facility for US Army special weapon systems during the Cold War though. We were given on-post army officer housing within a few weeks on the shore of Seneca Lake. I was able to get rides to and from work with other officers as needed until I was able to pay cash for an old Ford Maverick. We lived in this house by the lake for about two years. Our marriage finally began to improve slightly when we started going to church at Calvary Chapel of the Finger Lakes in Canandaigua, NY. We were still struggling, but I was finally starting to learn about God's awesome grace in a way that I might begin to grasp it.

I worked as a security platoon leader in the 295th. We were responsible for securing the storage and movement of army special weapons at Seneca Army Depot. This was necessarily a very elaborate operation. I learned that there were sixty five men and women in my new platoon during my first day on the job. The work schedule involved three "twelve hour" daytime guard shifts that kept me on duty for fifteen hours each as a platoon leader. These were followed by three administrative "eight hour" day shifts. We then worked three "twelve hour" overnight guard shifts that again took fifteen hours for me to complete. We were given three days off after each of these nine day cycles. It seemed I was again working almost all the time. I was always exhausted. The army sent me through some valuable security operations and management training programs while I was stationed at Seneca.

I was served with documents at the beginning of the year in 1987 requiring me to appear in court at Seneca Falls, NY. I was being sued for back child support that

I allegedly owed for the care and maintenance of my oldest daughter, Cathy. I had not been able to find my ex-wife or my daughter for the preceding three years. I had not immediately filed criminal charges for kidnapping when they disappeared because I had such a negative opinion of my own home life and ability to care for my daughter. I was resigned to the loss in the tacit belief that Cathy was better off with her mother wherever she was. It was too late to file the charges when I finally realized how wrong I was. The authorities would consider my early failure to file a criminal complaint as an indication that the problem was actually a civil dispute.

I was unable to find my ex-wife and daughter until these papers were served on me in New York. I learned that my ex-wife had taken my daughter to the upper peninsula of Michigan where she had changed her own name by remarrying. She had been experiencing very hard times financially and had gone to the Michigan Department of Child Welfare to request assistance for herself and our daughter. She didn't realize that the State of Michigan would try to locate me and sue me for child support. Finding me was easy through the US Military worldwide locator service. I flew to Michigan and recovered my daughter with assistance from the local police department.

She had changed a great deal in three years. Cathy Anne was a beautiful and much taller little girl. I was ecstatic to have her back with me, but I understood that she would miss her mother. The cruelty of this situation was not lost on me. I just didn't know any way to make it better. The State of Michigan immediately dropped the suit against me when they realized that my daughter was legally supposed to be in my custody in the first place. Cathy settled in quickly, but there was an underlying tension in our home because my wife tended to treat her harshly as a step-child whether intentionally or not. Our two youngest children accepted her slowly.

Jennifer was a sweet spirited two year old princess. Gregory was a very precocious five year old adventurer. Our home life was better because we were in church, but there was still a great deal of tension. There was never enough money. We were forced to visit food pantries on several occasions just to make sure there was enough food for our family. I was always exhausted because of my duty schedule.

My wife expressed that she believed I was intentionally abandoning my family to spend excessive time at work. This had been true at one time. The long hours I worked now were beyond my control. My job involved a real world mission in the waning years of the Cold War. It was very serious business. I had betrayed her trust early in our marriage, and she never really got past that. She had little or no respect for me. I had done very little to change this from her point of view. She didn't really understand the army. She had no real idea what I was involved in while I was at work, and I was not at liberty to tell her. It probably wouldn't have made any difference if I had explained everything to her though. She didn't understand what our military was actually doing at that time in US history. The fact that I was involved in it would not have significantly changed anything for her. I was just gone a lot as far as she was concerned, and we had little or no money. I could barely stay awake long enough to watch the kids so that she could get a break when I was home. I find no fault with her for how she felt. It would probably suffice to say that life was very difficult for our entire family. We were still together, but just barely.

My pride and arrogance didn't always mesh well in the high pressure environment created while maintaining absolute security for priceless weapon systems. I tried to use the same management style that had worked for me as a sergeant earlier in my career. I became too familiar with the enlisted soldiers in my platoon as a lieutenant and failed to learn from the old proverb, "Familiarity breeds contempt". I was promoted to 1st lieutenant in the middle of 1987. The 295th had lost several commissioned officers by the end of that year. We were making things work while managing the four platoons with a captain and two lieutenants. This was a very large MP company with a normal compliment of over three hundred enlisted soldiers and six commissioned officers. The commander's duties remained the same because he was ultimately responsible for all company operations. This left me and the other lieutenant responsible for all the tasks normally handled by five lieutenants.

The stress was high, and I didn't handle it well. I made a few judgment errors that would have seemed inconsequential in a civilian environment. They were considered serious for a junior army officer though. I had been given nearly maximum ratings on my officer evaluation reports early in my career. My company commander did a special officer evaluation report in December 1987 regarding my performance. He gave me a three out of five score on this report in the category of judgment. This would normally have had the effect that he intended by getting my attention directed toward correcting my own performance. This document, unfortunately, was included with my records when my promotion packet for the rank of captain was sent in a few months later. This was during a time when the army was reducing the number of company grade officers and preparing for a round of reduction in forces (budget cut) discharges. This single evaluation report was seen as a negative in my packet although the rest of my records were quite good. Any negative item at this time was enough to reject a promotion packet. I was passed over for promotion.

I was transferred from the 295th to a staff position in the Depot Directorate of Law Enforcement and Security at the beginning of 1988 when replacement officers were finally being sent to the company. The depot security operations officer was promoted to captain a few months later and transferred into the 295th to replace the company commander. I became his replacement as the new security operations officer. This new job made me directly responsible for security operations inside the "limited area" where the "special" weapons were stored and maintained. This meant that all the military police and DOD security personnel working in the "limited area" were under my operational control while they were on duty. I was responsible for all the security alarm devices, camera systems, electric fences, and security locking systems. The military police platoons from the 295th rotated in and out of the limited area in guard shifts. My office had a small enlisted clerical staff, a crew of three DOD alarm technicians, and a dedicated escort crew of military police personnel who protected the movement of weapon containers within the limited area between the storage igloos and the maintenance and assembly buildings.

We successfully went through several major inspections and operational challenges over the next year and a half. These successes were not enough to overcome the one negative report in my record, even though I subsequently received glowing evaluation reports from more senior officers. The post provost marshall and the post commander both tried to intervene on my behalf to no avail. The army had spent a tremendous amount of time and money training me for the duty that I was successfully performing. My training on heavy security and counter terrorism operations was extremely valuable and had cost a lot of taxpayer money.

My records packet was presented again to a promotion board in the spring of 1988. I was again passed over for promotion because of this single negative document which had been caused by my foolishness. The army has a very strict "up or out" policy for junior officers. I stayed on active duty until July of 1989 when I was given a reduction in forces (RIF) bonus, an Army Accommodation Medal, and an honorable discharge. This should have been the kind of experience that would humble me to the point of real change in my personal attitudes and behavior. I believe that it did have that effect for a short time as I struggled to find a civilian job over the next several months. I experienced a growing prideful bitterness as time passed that again negatively impacted all my thoughts and decisions.

We purchased a reliable car in New York with part of the RIF bonus. The army paid for a Ryder truck that we loaded with all of our household belongings. We were soon on our way to my parent's home in Missouri where I intended to get a fresh start at a career in heavy industrial security or law enforcement. I now had good professional credentials along with a massive chip on my shoulder. I had no real idea how tough the job market was because I had been in one form of government service or another for most of the past seven years. We had the remaining funds from the RIF bonus, but we had no idea that we would need most of that money to live on for the next six months.

The job search initially led me to a new alarm company in Springfield, Missouri. I was hired as a salesman. I learned a great deal about the commercial alarm industry during this brief employment, but I was not able to sell anything for about two months. It's obvious that God was moving in several ways to get my attention and call me to Himself. I just wasn't getting it. I had a very long road of turmoil and grief ahead for me and my family.

An opportunity soon developed for me to meet with a man who was the principal owner and CEO of a very large midwestern insulation company. This gentleman inherited the company from his parents and then spent thirty years working very hard to grow it into a successful industry powerhouse. He became a wealthy man with a well earned reputation for business sense mixed with generosity.

I had a vague idea regarding the potential for contract security management services in industrial environments. I believed that the nature of this particular company with its combination of manufacturing, warehousing, and sales operations made it an ideal potential client. I also had what I believed to be a strong advantage in this situation because the owner's parents had been very close church friends of my maternal grandparents. Getting an appointment to speak with him was fairly easy in fact. I looked forward to presenting my ideas and believed that this was a very real opportunity to finally find some success in my new job.

It rained quite a bit on the day of this scheduled meeting. The rain finally slowed, but there was standing water everywhere. I was wearing my best dark suit that day with a white shirt and power tie. We had an appointment to meet after lunch at my prospective client's office near downtown. I started out of my office a little early because I desperately wanted to make a good impression. The rain had started again. I held my briefcase over my head in lieu of an umbrella and ran across the parking lot to my car. I stepped up onto a painted concrete curb and slipped as I reached the parking space. I fell on the side of my left leg, but somehow managed to keep my upper body out of the huge puddle next to the car. I brushed the dirty water off the leg of my dark suit pants as I stood up and inspected closely to see if I could still make myself presentable. I reasoned that I didn't have time to go home and change clothes. I didn't believe the dampness on my trouser leg showed badly, and I felt like making the appointment on time was the most important consideration. I straightened myself up as best I could in the front seat of the car and headed over to my prospective client's office.

The importance of this meeting had grown in my mind. I had become quite intimidated by the time I arrived. It seemed that I needed to use some of the courage I had learned so much about as a soldier and police officer.

Lifting my head and straightening my shoulders, I headed through the front doors with a determination that almost made me forget falling in the flooded parking lot. My potential customer's personal secretary was very business like and extremely polite. She told me that he was expecting me.

The sound of stifled mirth and quick intakes of breath should have been obvious as I passed people in my journey from the parking lot to the palatial offices of this very influential man. The secretary ushered me into the room and told me to sit at the conference table just inside the door. My family friend was working at a massively ornate desk at the far end of his huge office. He told me to make myself comfortable. He would be with me momentarily. The secretary offered refreshments with a fixed smile and then left the room. I sat there trying to collect my thoughts and mentally hone my presentation for a few minutes. He finally walked over and sat down at the head of the table. He then turned his full attention to what I had to say. I jumped right in and gave what I felt was a good presentation of perceived need and proposed solutions. He listened politely and asked questions. He made comments that led me to believe the opportunity here was very real. We spoke for almost an hour as I remember. He got up and showed me very politely to the door when the conversation ended.

The secretary still seemed to be looking at me in a strange way as I left the office. Heading downstairs with intent purpose, I considered how best to pursue this potentially lucrative business opportunity. A cool wind had started blowing by the time I reached the parking lot. The sudden feeling of cold air striking my body in a peculiar place brought my optimism to a shocking halt. I realized that my suit trousers were ripped at the seam in back from the belt line to the crotch. My white boxer shorts were being presented to the public with all of the waving clarity of a stark flag of surrender. The mortification I felt in that moment was overwhelming. This would be funny at some time in the distant future, but my sense of humor deserted me in that moment. I called the office and didn't return to work that day. Even this basic lesson in humility was lost on me at the time. We probably still had an opportunity to do business with this old friend of my family. I never found out because I never went back. I met him again about twenty years later at a charitable event. He had either forgotten about it, graciously chose not to mention it, or more likely never noticed my embarrassment in the first place.

My search for a better position continued during this time. The financial stress was growing and my fragile marriage was becoming even more challenged. I was able to spend a lot of time with my dad who was now the pastor of a small church in Strafford, Missouri. Dad reminded me of the call to ministry I felt when I was twenty two years old. He could see the obvious signs of rebellion that permeated everything I said and did at this point in my life. He observed our very difficult marital problems. Dad displayed an incredible amount of tact and grace. He and mom did everything they could to show me and my small family that they loved us unconditionally. They were doing this not just because they were my parents and my children's grandparents, but because they were following the clear instructions found in God's word. I became more and more frantic in my job search as the money began to run low.

My wife had former foster parents living in north Texas. It eventually seemed clear that we would have to move closer to a larger metropolitan area for any real hope of restarting my career. The Dallas metro area in Texas started to seem ever more appealing. We decided to move to Texas for better opportunities just before the end of the year. My wife's foster parents offered us the use of rooms in their large home in Bonham, Texas until I found a good job and we could get reestablished. I was soon searching the Dallas metro area for employment.

The job search finally succeeded when I found a job in January 1990 as the operations director at a large private investigation firm in north Dallas. This company specialized in pre employment screening and internal theft investigations for commercial clients. The company ran undercover investigators operating within their client companies as "regular employees". These very elaborate investigations usually lasted several months as the operative became embedded in the social structure among the employees of the client company. The information gained in this way was incredibly valuable to the client management teams.

We were hired one day by a very old family owned restaurant business in Dallas to investigate the apparent systematic internal theft of several hundred thousand dollars. I took a direct personal interest in this particular investigation, which went on for over a month but remained fruitless. All communication we had at first with the client in this case was channeled through the company's executive vice president (EVP). We began to suspect after several weeks that our efforts were being impaired or deliberately thwarted by this person. We held a private meeting with the client CEO to discuss the problem in detail. He decided to help us work more quietly through a clever ruse. He would publicly accuse us of ineptitude and "fire" us for failing in our investigation. We would then quietly redirect our efforts and pursue the investigation while answering directly to him covertly. We soon felt we had reason to believe that the EVP and the manager of the company's central commissary might be directly involved in the systematic theft.

We gathered as much information as we could and then showed up without notice at the corporate office and commandeered the company classroom to do direct interviews. We wanted to speak with the people we believed were most likely involved in the ongoing theft activities. We did intend to call the EVP in to speak with us, but we had not announced this intention to her or anyone else other than the CEO. The EVP was aware of who was in the building because we had been announced by the receptionist. I happened to walk past her office and noticed that she was sitting at her desk with her face in her hands. We interviewed a few other people and then decided to call the EVP in to talk with us. We were told that she had quickly packed up her personal belongings and left the building soon after our arrival. We did not have a chance to speak with her before she left. We heard that she was considering filing suit against us and her former employer a few weeks after she left. Her outlandish claim was that she had been wrongfully accused of theft and terminated. This simply confirmed our suspicion regarding her involvement in the theft activities.

She had departed on her own volition without any conversation between us.

Investigations often end this way. It is quite common
to reach a point where all of the available evidence in a
situation causes the investigator to form a theory that
can't be proven beyond a reasonable doubt. Fictional
detectives in books, movies, and television shows who
manage to "prove who did it" in most of their cases are
the product of their creators' imaginations. They bear
little resemblance to actual professional public and private investigators. Most real investigators often feel like
they are searching for a particular blade of grass in an
open field at night. They very rarely (if ever) reach a conclusion in which they are absolutely certain they have
uncovered the complete truth. This is why our founding
fathers insisted on including the "presumption of innocence" in our constitution. They knew from bitter experience with the European legal systems of their day that
protecting the freedom of the common man required
the burden of proof to be heaviest for the state when
criminal prosecutions were processed.

The actions of the suspected executive vice president
solidified our suspicions when she left the company that
day. She didn't have to say anything. No criminal prosecution was pursued in this case. The company was never
able to recover the stolen funds. The largely unexplained
losses seemed to virtually stop though after the investigation was closed and the suspected parties were no
longer employed by the company.

The same restaurant company later hired me upon
release from the PI firm. I became their loss control
director. We moved our family to the Garland area at this

time because the commute from Bonham to Dallas every morning was too far and too expensive. Our finances were even more dismal than they had been. My struggle with pride, selfishness, and arrogance were worse than ever although I had started to realize that most of the problems were my own fault. My wife and I fought with each other almost constantly. My children were exposed to all kinds of things that they should have never seen. Everything in our family life just continued to deteriorate. We eventually settled in Rockwall, TX.

My employment with the restaurant company lasted for about a year and half while I pursued opportunities at the same time to work on random cases with a local private investigator I had come to know. My duties with my employer were increasingly moving in the direction of food service management and away from the law enforcement and security career I thought I still wanted.

There were some very interesting and influential men involved with this restaurant company on the board of directors. The company itself was over 70 years old. It had been a Dallas fixture for many decades with locations spread around the city. The CEO was married to the daughter of the original company founders. He was a lawyer by training, but he had been running the restaurant company for about thirty years. This man was firmly entrenched in the Dallas First Baptist Church. In fact, his Sunday school teacher was the famous motivational speaker, Zig Ziglar. The board of directors included Jack Page (of Page Pharmacies), A. W. Cullum (the founder of Tom Thumb Grocery Stores), and noted theologian Dr. Charles Ryrie of the Dallas Theological Seminary. I even received a Ryrie Study Bible from Dr. Ryrie with a hand written inscription from him directing me to John 17:17.

God had planted me in this company for His own purposes and for my family's good, but I was too stupid and prideful to understand. I continued to long for the perceived "greener grass" and freedom I thought existed in the life of my friends who were private detectives. I decided to leave the restaurant company in the early winter of 1992 and start my own business as a private investigator. I didn't consult God in this situation. I didn't consult my wife or my parents. I told my wife what I was going to do and ignored her when she disagreed with me.

The CEO of the restaurant company told me one day that he was grooming me to take an active role in managing the company after his retirement. He shared this information on the day I gave my two week notice. He told me that he had come to think of me as one of his sons. He was completely shocked with my decision to leave. This very kind old gentleman told me, with tears in his eyes, that he would honor my two week notice. He explained that he wanted me to think diligently every day of those two weeks with the hope that I would come to my senses. I felt horrible, but I had made up my mind to leave, and I followed through with my incredibly stupid plan.

Chapter 11

Explosively Redeemed

"Come now, let us reason together, says the LORD:
though your sins are like scarlet,
they shall be as white as snow;
though they are red like crimson,
they shall become like wool."
(Isaiah 1:18)

The State of Texas licensed me as a private investigator in 1992. We soon learned what a huge mistake I had made. There were periods when we made quite a large amount of money. There were even longer times when we endured near starvation. We got involved in everything from family law investigations to property recoveries and process service. I continued to rebel and run away from the plan God had for me. The further I sank into rebellion, the worse things got at home and in business.

Our finances had, once again, reached the point of essential bankruptcy by the middle of 1993. Our marriage was holding together by a mere thread of dogged determination. Our children were suffering from lack of provision compounded by the lack of an effective father and the rampant conflict between their parents. I told my dad about all of it in a telephone conversation. He listened patiently and then suggested that we move our family and the business to Missouri. He would again help us get on our feet financially and emotionally. We agreed and soon moved back to Missouri. We didn't file for bankruptcy protection again, but we might as well have. We started a new PI company in Polk County with help from my parents. We rented a duplex from an old school friend and moved to Bolivar where I had graduated from high school in 1975.

We began, at first, to earn a pretty good living doing all types of operations including criminal defense support, internal theft probes, insurance fraud cases, family law, and divorce investigations. I had been using closed circuit television equipment periodically over the preceding few years. This technology was part of my formal training and heavy security operations I had been involved with in the army. We added small camera system installations to our business to help fill in the slow times.

The same fraternal benefit society I had worked for sixteen years earlier took me back on a part time basis when the economy began to slow down in 1995. Our marriage continued to deteriorate, and my personal behavior followed suit. I began again to find any excuse possible for being anywhere but home. I was tormented by my own pride and fear of failure while I was driven by my flesh and the enemy to seek relief and self aggrandizement wherever I thought I could find it. I sank to new depths in loss of integrity and the pursuit of what I thought was happiness. My wife had no reason to trust me because I was obviously untrustworthy. My children could not count on me because whenever I was home I was fighting with their mother. This was destroying my family, but I had become so self absorbed that I was almost completely blind to the pain of those around me. I began to abuse alcohol in the same way I had decades earlier. My business became so bad that financial ruin was once again a single misstep away.

Dad finally reached the end of his patience. He came to my home one night with both of my brothers and confronted me in the driveway. I said awful things to my dear father that night. I could see the look of hurt, grief, and anger in his eyes as I told him I regretted being his son. This confrontation almost devolved into a physical fight with my brothers. The police were called to my residence, and they forced my father and brothers to leave. That was the last time I spoke with my dad for over two years.

It's difficult to consider how morally low I had gone, or how much lower I would sink in the near future. I often desperately wish I could go back and undo these cruel things, but life doesn't work like that. It's important, while writing this now, to remember that there is a purpose here greater than my personal comfort. There is a temptation to stop right here out of revulsion caused by memories from my past. Thank God for his awesome grace! He never gave up on me, and neither did my dad. I never stopped being my fathers' son whether I wanted to or not.

We reached the point where we simply couldn't keep going in business on our own any longer in January of 1997. One of the CCTV equipment distributors I had been using hired me as a salesman. The Lord blessed me with good sales and I was finally able to pay some of my bills. A new camera distributor, Global Technologies, offered me a better position in March of the same year. This company was staffed by some of my acquaintances who saw that I had a propensity for selling this type of equipment. I was offered a pay increase and I jumped at the opportunity. Global Technologies employed me selling camera components and doing installation work for them for the next seven years. I began selling used medical endoscopy equipment to veterinarians as a side business at the same time. The experience at Global Technologies greatly enhanced my understanding of camera systems and closed circuit television installation through intense study and direct application.

Our home life was now very bad. I realized there was a real danger of my wife and I killing each other if we didn't get apart. We had been married almost seventeen years. My daughter Cathy left home one night at age seventeen during a particularly bad fight and didn't come back. My son Greg was fifteen and my youngest daughter Jennifer was twelve. I had reached a place emotionally and spiritually where I felt like I belonged in the sewer. I owed money to almost everyone I knew. I couldn't tell the truth if it slapped me in the face. I had become the most despicable and untrustworthy person in my life. The simple term depression is not adequate to describe my mental state at this time. The living disaster that I had become was much more complicated and filthy than that term implies. I didn't blame my wife for all of my problems, and I still don't. It seemed clear that even worse disaster was inevitable if the marriage did not end. It was obvious that the near constant turmoil my children had seen and endured to this point could at least be ended if I left.

I moved out of the rental house we were occupying and moved into a basement apartment alone. It was in an older complex that is located directly across the street from the National Cemetery in Springfield, Missouri. The price was right, and the location fit my lifestyle and mindset. My marriage ended in divorce soon afterward. I agreed to pay fifteen hundred dollars per month in child support because I knew my ex-wife couldn't earn a living wage and I wanted my children to be taken care of. My financial circumstances immediately became worse. I found myself doing even more crooked things in my fight to stay ahead in this rolling disaster. I was raised better than this. My life was now full of things that I never would have done had my perverse "situational ethics" not allowed me to rationalize my behavior.

A young man who owned a check collection company in Springfield wanted to become a private investigator. He hired me in late 1997 to teach him the PI business while I was in the middle of this personal storm. I tried to dissuade him at first, but his mind was set on this plan. I finally agreed to teach him. In the process I became acquainted with his office manager, Patti.

I was so burnt out at this time that any ability I might have had to appreciate true beauty or value was almost gone. Patti was like a beautiful diamond among the ashes even in my weary self inflicted fog. We spent a great deal of time talking together over the next several months. We talked about everything, anything, and nothing at all. We found that we could share our deepest secrets, hopes, dreams, and fears without any dread, recrimination, or judgment. The more we got to know one another, the closer we became. It seemed like we were kindred spirits of sorts because our lives were so similarly messed up. Patti was like none of the women I had been involved with in the past. She lived with a refined sweetness that was clearly neither false nor temporary even though she had been through very difficult times of her own.

Patti was beautiful from the inside out regardless of the circumstances. I would have been blind not to see the marked contrast between her and so many other young women with beauty that covers the surface but obscures their true nature. She was recently divorced. Her life had been very similar to mine. Her marriage ended one morning during a particularly dangerous and stressful incident in which the police had to intervene to help her leave home with her youngest daughter Pamela. Patti's son Nathan and her oldest daughter Kelly had already left home and had children of their own.

Patti seemed to be a beacon of normalcy and stability to me, but I was very resistant to making any kind of commitment in my self-absorbed mindset. We became very close friends in the middle of the storm. We were soon living together although I continued to maintain a separate apartment.

Greg called me one day after a few months in his mother's home without me there. He begged to come and live with me. I happily said yes and he moved into my basement apartment right before Christmas. My youngest daughter Jennifer was a beautiful and tender-hearted twelve year old at the time her mother and I separated. I know that the break up of her parent's marriage had a devastating effect on her. If there was some way I could go back and undo the harm that I inflicted on my children through my selfishness I would do it instantly. However, as I've already observed, life doesn't work like that.

Some people have a tough time learning that decisions we make so casually in a moment can have a life-long shattering impact on those we hold most dear. The simple fact is that the Bible is true. We do reap what we sow. Unfortunately, our children innocently share in the pain at harvest time. I was gone when Jennifer needed me most during her teen years. My daughter Cathy went back to North Carolina to be near her mother. Jennifer and her mother stayed in Missouri for a short time and then moved back to Texas. I essentially lost contact with Jennifer for the next couple of years because she would not agree to visit with me the way I was living. I clearly understand now how she must have felt. Those years are gone and they can never be recovered. Jennifer has felt abandoned by me ever since. I pray that God will repair the damage I inflicted on this precious young lady in the way that only He can.

My son desperately needed a dad to teach him right from wrong and help him through the very difficult teenage years. What he got instead was me. I practically abandoned him after he came to live with me as I continued to strive for whatever I selfishly wanted at the time. It's not just that he essentially raised himself. I had become an alcoholic by this time. Greg was often left alone to his own devices. My bizarre lifestyle made alcohol and other harmful things readily available. He needed me to grow up and start teaching him how to live as a responsible adult. I was too busy. He needed me to teach him how to love a woman. I was too busy. He needed me to teach him how to handle money. I was too busy. He needed me to teach him about God. I was in total rebellion.

Greg reached age sixteen and I finally realized that I hadn't really taught him anything useful. It occurred to me that he needed to learn a trade. He had been helping me in the camera business on and off for a couple of years and I recognized that he had a technical aptitude. One of my friends was a very talented CCTV installer. I had worked with this man for a few years and he was currently doing installation work for Global Technologies as a subcontractor. I asked him to take Greg on as an apprentice, and he told me that he couldn't afford to pay him. It was understood that Greg wouldn't agree to work without pay just to gain experience. I offered to pay his hourly wage if my friend would pass the money on to him. We wanted Greg to get paid so that he would participate willingly and gain confidence as he learned the trade.

The problem with this plan was that I didn't explain very well what I was doing and why. Greg thought the whole effort was just some machination on my part to get rid of him when it came out that I had been paying his wages. When he started driving, he had several accidents and I made his life even worse by replacing each car he wrecked at first instead of making him face the tough losses life would throw at him. Greg started predictably to get into trouble as he neared adulthood.

I finally went to dad early in 1999 and humbly apologized for all that I had done and said to him. He readily forgave me. We became very close again in the final year and a half of his life. He met Patti and liked her immediately. My parents were living in rural Buffalo, Missouri at this time. Patti and I tried to go and see them each weekend for a few hours. Dad's health had deteriorated significantly. He was struggling with the congestive heart failure that would eventually take his life.

Dad continued to be the man of God I had known since childhood even in these difficult days as he labored to breathe. The difference between my life and his was striking. He had far outlived the predictions of his Chicago doctors. He sometimes acted short with Mom as she worked to care for him, but he loved her completely, loved his children resolutely, and loved Jesus totally. He told Patti and me on one occasion, as he fought for breath, that he didn't understand why he couldn't just go home to be with Jesus. We understood that he was exhausted. He finally succumbed to the chronic coronary artery disease that had plagued him for over 35 years on December 18, 2000. The funeral was sad, but it was also a celebration of his life and his entry into heaven. Mom was understandably devastated. She continued to live in the house in rural Buffalo. We made it a point to visit with her every Sunday afternoon for the next couple of years.

Greg turned eighteen in 2000. I again tried to influence him toward something that I believed would be good for him. I took him to the army recruiter's office.

The army readily accepted him in the middle of November and he was sent to Ft. Benning, Georgia for basic training, infantry school, and jump school. The army allowed Greg to come home on leave to attend his grandfather's funeral. He then returned to Ft. Benning and worked his way through the rest of his training. Greg's mother and I were able to attend his graduation from Infantry School.

Patti and I attended his graduation about a month later from the US Army Parachute School. The army allowed me to pin my son's jump wings on his chest as a former paratrooper honoring a brand new one in one of the greatest moments of my life to that point. Greg was scheduled to attend the ranger induction program and was assigned to the school immediately after he completed parachute training. The army had difficulty filling the class though. This resulted in repeated "filler weeks". Anyone who has experienced the disjointed waiting and slave like details of a trainee waiting in a "filler week" will understand that pulling grass blades out of sidewalk cracks and doing endless police calls every day can get very old very fast.

Greg called me one day to let me know that he had had enough. He asked me where I thought the army would send him if he withdrew from the ranger program. We soon learned that he would be sent to Ft. Bragg, NC. We knew that this probably meant assignment to the 82nd Airborne Division, but we were both very surprised when he ended up in the same battalion that I had first joined in 1975. Greg was assigned to C Company, 2nd Battalion, 325th Parachute Infantry Regiment. I had been in A Company of the same battalion and regiment. It was very strange when I learned that he now lived in the barracks next door to the one I had lived in twenty five years earlier.

My life was now the discordant existence of an aging rebel. We had been selling a lot of equipment and making a considerable amount of money, but we had nothing to show for it. Most of the money I made was being wasted on my hedonistic lifestyle. The rest was sent to my ex-wife or paid to a growing number of frustrated creditors. God allowed me at the same time, ironically, to continue developing a wealth of knowledge on the installation and use of closed circuit video equipment.

We had extensively used security camera equipment in the army. I continued to use camera equipment as a private investigator. We had been selling and installing CCTV systems and components for several years. I was now teaching this technology to others as we continued to sell the equipment all over the country. I was at the same time pursuing ways to adapt industrial camera components with used medical endoscopy equipment for veterinary endoscopy. A lot of this work was done for other companies as I continued to work in the security side of the camera industry. I soon began selling these hybrid systems directly to veterinary practices without any real character or loyalty. There was a need for this type of equipment in the veterinary industry and most veterinarians could not afford to purchase new medical grade equipment. God, in his grace, allowed me to succeed in this area for a season.

Many of these transactions and most of my business relationships were handled in the same cavalier self serving fashion I had used throughout my adult life to that point. I made and squandered a small fortune in a short period of time. We ended up with nothing more than technical expertise, deeper debt, and a growing list of angry disappointed customers, vendors, and family members. My abuse of alcohol was out of control. Practical loyalty to anyone in my life was almost nonexistent. I was an angry self absorbed loser with no self respect and almost no respect for anyone else. Patti and I continued to visit with mom on Sunday afternoons, and God continued to shine his light into my dark world through the gracious patient love I saw in my saintly mother.

The world changed again before our eyes on September 11, 2001. We watched in shock while Islamic terrorists crashed airplanes into the World Trade Center, the Pentagon, and a forlorn field in the Pennsylvania countryside. Our country was again at war whether we understood it or not. I was very concerned about Greg. I was acutely aware of the mission his unit would most likely be given in any planned retaliation. I knew he would be deployed somewhere in the world as our nation reacted to this cowardly attack with an immediate resolve to strike back. In a very strange way, the beginning of the terror wars brought me out of my downward spiral slightly while I began to worry about my son and daughters.

There was a growing national patriotism for most of the people in America at this time, unlike the national experience with Vietnam. There were, as always, a relatively small number of US citizens who possessed an irrational hatred of our free market economy and democratic institutions that made them cry out against anything that would magnify American exceptionalism or self defense. Most people were appalled by the brutality of the attacks, and inspired by the hundreds of courageous acts that we learned about on the part of the first responders to each attack site.

We began seeing an overwhelming outpour of patriotic sentiment as President Bush brought the country onto a war footing. The contrast was striking to anyone who had seen the Vietnam War protests in the summer of 1968. We listened to thousands of young people in city streets chanting "USA, USA, USA". Military recruiting offices were immediately overwhelmed with young men and women wanting to join. There was a sense that the jihadists had made the same mistake the Japanese had made at Pearl Harbor, Hawaii in 1941. They had awakened a sleeping giant. We were coming for them and we were furious.

Mom began to ask Patti and I to visit a new church she had been attending in Ozark, Missouri called James River Assembly as 2002 came and went. She was pretty insistent about this without being difficult in any way. We heard the same invitation almost every Sunday afternoon. I was having none of it at first. I remember telling Patti as we drove down the highway one afternoon that there was no way I was going to go to church. The sick reprobate that I had become went on to say something pathetic like, "if I decide to go to a social club, we'll join the YMCA".

Mom continued to patiently ask. We now know that she also continued to cry out to God in prayer on our behalf. I love mom very much and this was still true even in my desperate moral condition. She was still grieving the loss of our dad. We couldn't help feeling compassion for her in her loneliness. It would be reasonable to think that I also felt some degree of guilt. My conscience was so seared and my heart was so hard at that point, however, that I don't believe it would be true.

God continued to allow my circumstances to become increasingly more desperate. I lived in an almost constant state of anger and deep depression. God was working powerfully, as only He can, to bring me to the end of myself as Christmas came and went that year. We finally decided to surrender to the tender pleas of my dear mother when the holiday season came to a close. We agreed that we would go to church with her once on a Sunday morning to try and satisfy her. It did make her visibly happy when we told her we would go.

I owed money to virtually everyone I knew at this point in my life. These were debts that I could never possibly repay. I was completely ensnared in my own selfishness, pride, anger, and addictions. I was a liar and a thief. I had been divorced twice and was separated from my children who were truly better off for the separation. I was angry, violent, and dangerous to those around me. I saw no future, no hope, and no real purpose for myself. I believe the only thing that prevented my suicide was God's amazing grace. In my case, His grace took the form of a clear understanding that hell was waiting for me when I took my last breath.

The fateful Sunday of our first James River visit arrived in the middle of January, 2003. We entered the huge church building and found seats in the very back of the balcony area as far away from the pulpit as possible while still being inside the place. The music started and the choir began to sing. The song was a good one and I glanced over to see what Patti thought about it. She was crying and tears were streaming down her face. I was soon shocked to find that I was crying too. Pastor John Lindell stepped up to the microphone when the music stopped and began to deliver one of the clearest expositional messages I had ever heard. He was teaching right out of the book of 1st Corinthians in the New Testament.

There might as well have been no one else in the auditorium within a few minutes because Pastor Lindell was talking straight to me. It's now quite clear that this was God talking to me through Pastor Lindell. We said goodbye to mom and went home when the service ended. We talked a lot about the message at home that day and decided to go back the next week. We experienced the same phenomenon on the next Sunday morning. As soon as we got home from church on that second Sunday, Patti and I went into our room, and fell to our knees. I don't know how long we prayed, but I know we both poured out all our sin, pain, anger, and desperation at the Awesome Feet of Jesus Christ, the King of Kings.

There was no "cleaning up" accomplished before we finally surrendered to Christ. We had clearly made no real effort to change before this happened, but our lives would never be the same afterward. The changes in me were so drastic and profound that they shocked me and everyone around me. The same changes occurred in Patti. We were aware that our desires were different. Everything was new. Where there had been hatred, there was now love that was far greater and more real than our limited ability to understand. Where depression had ruled, there was now a deep and growing joy that was put there by God. Where there had been no hope, there was a plan and a purpose greater than we could have ever imagined on our own. Where there had been anger, there was now peaceful compassion and kindness that seemed strange but somehow very right. Where there had been deceitfulness, there was now a deep appreciation for the truth and a passionate desire to live in it. Where there had been addiction, there was now growing stability and self control.

We began to pray together and read the Bible together when we woke up in the morning and before we went to sleep at night. Addictions which seemed impossible to let go of weeks earlier simply lost there appeal and importance. We were having a conversation about our new life a few days later and realized that we needed to follow through with some very important decisions. We both understood that we had been rescued from ourselves through faith in Jesus and his awesome sacrifice. Patti understood grace a lot better than I did at this time, but I was learning quickly.

We decided that we needed to start taking steps to grow in our relationship with God as he led us out of the dark hole we had been in for so long. We decided to start with just one more good decision and see what might happen next. We agreed that living together like we were was wrong. It was now February of 2003. We were armed with this new resolve when we took a late lunch hour on Valentine's Day and went to the county courthouse where we were married by a circuit court judge. We knew that Greg would soon be on his way to Iraq. Our honeymoon consisted of a quick trip to Ft. Bragg with our nephew Zachary to see Greg before he left on his impending deployment. The Iraq war had not yet started, but we knew it was inevitable. Greg couldn't discuss it, but I knew he would soon be in the middle of a ferocious fight.

We continued to attend church at James River. The people there were amazing. They welcomed us into their church family as if we were a long lost brother and sister. The love we felt among them was genuine yet difficult to describe. The pastor continued to teach from the Bible line by line, and we were absorbing it like sponges. We were learning very rapidly about King Jesus and His plan for our lives. Patti and I continued to start and end each day reading the Bible and praying together. Old bad habits continued to fall away. We were not perfect and we still aren't, but we were forgiven and freed from slavery to the dark and treacherous lifestyle we had been enmeshed in for so long. We were really learning how to live again. The more we learned, the more involved we became in church.

We were taught at James River that God loves us absolutely and that he paid the Highest Price ever paid to give us the Greatest Gift ever given. We were taught that we could succeed because the best was yet to come, and God would always see us through the difficulties and trials we still had to face. We got involved in an excellent adult bible fellowship class called The Journey. The people in the class treated us like we were family. They drew us into the real church in a way that showed us we were accepted just as we were. Then they challenged us to become what God planned for us to be. We decided to become members of James River Assembly within a couple of years. I couldn't help laughing at myself when

I remembered the buffoon I had been spouting my "wise" ideas regarding the merits of "joining a social club". We discovered that this was way better than "joining the YMCA"!

Greg's unit was deployed at the start of the war, but they didn't actually enter Iraq until the beginning of April in the attack on the Iraqi air force base at Talil. They were decisively involved after that in the battle at As Samawa, and in several other cities along the way to Bagdad. When Bagdad fell, they occupied a part of the city for about seven months before being moved to a new position at the airport. We spent long hours praying for them, watching news reports, and searching for information on the internet. We didn't hear from Greg for over thirty days after he deployed. We were tremendously relieved to learn that he was alright when we were finally able to communicate with him. We tried to write to him very often and ended up sending him three or four letters per week. During one of the early satellite phone calls I had with him, he asked me to send him small amounts of cash whenever possible concealed inside my letters. He also asked us to send care packages containing everything from campers toilet paper to candy and snack foods. Patti and I collected and sent these small boxes often. We also started including ten to fifteen dollars cash with every letter we sent to him.

We felt like we were contributing to Greg's well being and doing our part to help him. I would like to believe that the packages and the cash helped him to stay encouraged and hopeful. With every letter, I also sent small portions of scripture that I believed would reach him with the love of Jesus. I had learned from

Isaiah 55 that "God's Word does not return to Him void." "It accomplishes what He sent it to do". James River had a vigorous military support program that included praying for and sending care packages to our service men and women involved in the war. We were not the only people praying for their safe return. Our church family adopted Greg and prayed for him intensely during this very difficult period.

One of our most common prayers was that God would blind and confuse the enemy and cause the enemy's weapons and plans to malfunction. Greg later told us of numerous incidents when he was protected from almost certain injury or death. He was deployed for eleven months. It sometimes seemed as if we were just sending letters and things out with no real response. Greg had every letter I had sent him when returned from this deployment. They were wrapped with plastic inside a container with a camouflage pattern Bible he had received from an army chaplain.

Patti and I drove to Ft. Bragg to meet Greg's unit when they returned from Iraq in early March of 2004. The company was delayed several days in Germany on their way back to the US. We spent some time with Greg's former barracks roommate, Joe Bailey, while we waited. Joe had been sent back wounded after the battle at As Samawa. We learned a great deal about the early days of the war from our conversations with Joe.

We were at the barracks one morning while we waited, and we got into a conversation with the young sergeant on Charge of Quarters duty. The sergeant was sitting at a desk in the entrance to the building. He was wearing an immaculately clean and pressed BDU uniform. This cheerful young man was extremely courteous and businesslike. I asked him why he had come back early from the deployment. He explained that he had been "injured" as if it was an insignificant issue. The conversation continued until a telephone on the wall started ringing. The phone was several feet away from the desk. This young hero stood up to answer it and bent over to pick up the cane he needed to walk across the room. I was shocked to see the horrific burn scars that ran from the back of his head down his neck and into the top of his shirt collar as he passed me. I felt like weeping as I wondered where our country was able to find champions like this.

We were in a hangar at Pope Air Force Base the next morning and watched as Greg and the rest of his company arrived back in the US after a combat deployment of almost a year. We didn't know what would happen next. We were just overwhelmed with gratitude for answered prayers that included their safe return. Greg came home on leave a few weeks later. We persuaded him to wear his class-A uniform and go to church with us on that first Sunday morning. He reluctantly agreed. I let the church know he would be there. The music service ended that morning, and one of the pastors announced that there was a special visitor in the building. He then introduced Greg as a young man that our church had been praying for while he had been fighting in Iraq. The pastor asked Greg to stand. Almost 3000 people in the auditorium rose to their feet as he stood up and began applauding in a thunderous roar. This ovation went on for almost a minute. I watched with tears streaming down my face as my new church family welcomed my son. The war went on, but for now Greg was home.

Patti and I continued to grow in our relationship with Christ and with each other. We both became increasingly dissatisfied with our current jobs over the next several months. I was tired of selling and wanted to start working exclusively as a camera installer. Greg and I had discussed starting a new company in a partnership when he returned from the army, but that would have to wait until he got out. Patti and I believed we needed to do something different right away. She had been helping me with camera installations occasionally and I knew that I could teach her to be an effective technician. We both left our jobs in mid July, 2004, with God's grace, and started a new camera installation service company. The company began on "a shoe string" as they say. God blessed it though. We were soon very busy. We eventually had more work than we could handle and the company started to grow. I learned several lessons during this period about my own imperfections and made several business mistakes. We also found that God's grace is immeasurably more powerful than my propensity for being stupid. Our business prospered regardless of my errors.

We got involved in discipleship ministries at James River and worked for several years in the Discovery Class where we met you Troy. We worked in the altar ministry at the same time. We became Life Group leaders when James River started this house church ministry. We've been engaged in these and other ministries for the past decade. It's been a tremendous blessing to work with people as they escaped the dark sinister world of the enemy and surrendered their lives to Christ.

Our company was absorbed by our largest customer, CoLiant Solutions, Inc. at the end of 2008. CoLiant Solutions is owned by a dynamic Christian couple named Ken and Contessa Stallings. I have found an employment home and extended family in CoLiant. A few years ago, Ken allowed me to volunteer as the company chaplain. I've made no secret of my Christianity and I occasionally have opportunities to pray with coworkers.

My youngest daughter Jennifer lives in north Texas near her mother. I don't believe she has ever fully forgiven me for allowing our family to break apart when she was a child. I pray that she will soon accept my apology and see our relationship restored to what it should have been.

My son Greg lives in southwest Missouri with his beautiful new wife Kitty. I don't see or hear from Greg, but I pray that he too will forgive me soon. I love my children very much, but I've found that there is a heavy price to pay for the kind of life I've led. Even though God forgives us and removes our sin debt, we still reap the seeds we have sown.

My oldest daughter Cathy and I now have a friendship that has continued to mature as I've changed and grown in my walk with Jesus. She now lives in Georgia with her children. We don't get to see them often, but we love them very much. The same is true with my step children Pamela, Kelly, and Nathan. Their father died several years ago. We know that I can never replace him as their dad. However, we have become very good friends, and to their children I'm Grandpa Dave. It still seems like it would be great if I could somehow go back and undo all my mistakes. God doesn't allow that of course, but He does take things the way they are and make all of them work together for our good when we are completely sold out to Him.

Gratitude displaces pride in much the same way that light displaces darkness. I'm fascinated and humbled to remember that God called me to ministry when I was 22 years old. I rebelled and ran away like Jonah in my foolishness and pride. Jesus, in His awesome grace, came after me and brought me back. I think about the passage of scripture that says, "The gifts and calling of God are irrevocable." (Romans 11:29) I realize that this is true even for me. It seems to me like He is making up for all of the time that I wasted.

Chapter 12

Redemptive Echoes

"Truly, truly, I say to you,
whoever hears My word and believes Him who sent Me
has eternal life. He does not come into judgment,
but has passed from death to life."
(John 5:24)

Writing my personal story has given me a very strange perspective. It's almost as if I've been able to view that story as an outsider looking into it. God's sovereign grace seems even more awesome from that point of view. I was born into a Christian home to honest and devout Christian parents. I was taught the gospel message from a very early age and given every opportunity to absorb the miraculous nature of that message. My parents loved each other dearly, loved their children sacrificially, and loved Jesus completely. My brothers and my sister were not only my siblings, they were my friends. The home that I grew up in was not broken. My family was supportive in every possible way. It makes almost no sense to me, in light of these facts, that I would go through the self inflicted sorrow and pain that my rebellion later caused.

Jesus told a parable about the Word of God being like seed being sown by a farmer. He said, "A sower went out to sow his seed. And as he sowed, some fell along the path and was trampled under foot, and the birds of the air devoured it. And some fell on the rock, and as it grew up, it withered away, because it had no moisture. And some fell among thorns, and the thorns grew up with it and choked it. And some fell into good soil and grew up and yielded a hundredfold" (Luke 8:5-8). Jesus was talking about what happened in my life with regard to God's Word. I feel like I could be a poster boy for all of these different soil types.

I learned all the Bible stories when I was very young. I listened to sermon after sermon. I was exposed to the truth of the gospel in a consistent repetitive way that should have made it easy for me to grasp. My parents insisted that I go to church when I was young. I wanted to please them, and I wanted to fit in with my family. This is apparently a very common experience for children raised in church.

It's easy for a person to be immersed in church without actually belonging to the church. This is like "couch surfing" in God's house without actually belonging to His family. This religious thing is certainly not new. It's been around since the days of Adam and Eve. There are thousands of religions in the world even now in fact. The interesting thing about all these religions is that every one of them includes something the person has to do or not do in order to be accepted by the deity or object of worship. Even in Christian churches, there are countless people who are going through all the motions and trying to live up to the religious standards and rules that they believe will earn them a place in heaven. These people are not relying on the grace of God. They actually believe it's possible for them to somehow be "good" enough to be accepted by God in His Awesome Holiness.

There are other people in church who don't care about the one true God at all. They are only there for show. They don't really care about truly following religious rules, but they want to impress other people. They act like they are holy so that they can pridefully enjoy all the real or perceived benefits of belonging to the church. These people would never surrender any of their personal "rights", but outwardly they look righteous! Jesus described them this way, "Woe to you, scribes and Pharisees, hypocrites! you are like whitewashed tombs, which outwardly appear beautiful, but within are full of dead peoples bones and all uncleanness. So you also outwardly appear righteous to others, but within you are full of hypocrisy and lawlessness." (Matthew 23:27-28).

Think about it for a minute. All the Israelites walked across the bed of the Red Sea on dry ground when God parted the water so they could escape with Moses from the Egyptians. Yet, none of the adults who crossed the sea that day survived to enter the promise land except Joshua and Caleb. This was because Joshua and Caleb were the only adults who, along with Moses, really believed God and His promises. All the adult Israelites had seen the plagues God had placed on the Egyptians. They crossed the Red Sea on dry ground. They ate manna from heaven. They drank water that flowed out of the rock. They saw the pillar of cloud and the pillar of fire. God delivered and protected them as he gave them military victories. He fed them miraculously. He provided water for them miraculously. Their clothes and sandals didn't even wear out. It seems astounding that they didn't trust Him. He had proven Himself over and over again, but they died in the desert because of their unbelief.

There are many later examples of this failure to believe on the part of God's chosen people. God's people often rebelled in disbelief. He would allow their enemies to attack and subdue them when they rebelled. They would eventually realize what they had done and cry out to Him for mercy and deliverance. He would then raise up a leader who would be used to set them free from their oppressors. God then blessed them in every possible way, and they miraculously became wealthy and safe under His graceful care. They would gradually begin to slip back into the same old pattern of disloyalty, unbelief, and rebellion when this happened and the cycle would start over again. The stories in the Old Testament regarding the exploits of the great heroes of faith are almost all part of this recurring pattern.

Jesus had one man in His inner circle of disciples who participated in His ministry for three years without ever really becoming a member of Jesus' family. Judas was there for the sermons in front of huge crowds. He was there to enjoy the quiet evening discussions among small groups of close friends. Judas participated in the miracles. He was there when thousands were fed with small numbers of fish and loaves of bread. Judas was there when the blind were given sight, when the lame were made able to walk, and when the dead were brought back to life. Judas was there through it all. He saw it all. He heard it all. Yet, he still betrayed the Master.

My life was like that. I saw and heard the truth for years and kept rejecting it. The seed of the Word had fallen on rocky soil. I'm not alone in this. There are people like this of all ages in the church right now. They're just hanging out in the house with little or no real understanding of the looming disaster their unbelief will bring them. They don't appreciate the wonder and glory of the life Jesus has purchased for them. God amazingly never gives up on us though as long as we are still breathing.

The fact that I had to be in church so often as a child filled me with resentment. I heard warning after warning, and I cried out for mercy without offering surrender. My heart became progressively hardened rather than accepting the seed of the Word and growing fruitful. I felt trapped. I wanted to do my own thing. I had no depth emotionally or spiritually. It was easy for the enemy to come along and snatch the word away from me before it could come alive and grow. I began in rebellion to make my own plans and decisions as soon as I was old enough to do so.

It wasn't long before I realized that the consequences of my bad decisions were painful. My heart was like the rocky soil when I was in this mindset. The lessons I had been taught as a child came back to me and I reached for those truths in an insincere way seeking relief from my difficulties and pain. The word was revived and started to grow quickly, but it wasn't watered and didn't have any real chance to change me. It quickly withered without any care and died. I found myself hardened into an even worse state than before.

Rebellion continued to drag me deeper into the filth and depravity that I had almost started to accept as normal for me. Light filtered slowly into my dark world, and I was again brought to a place where I heard the Word. My pride and selfishness were so powerful, at this point; that the things I thought I wanted in life easily entangled me and choked out the Word. It had finally started to make sense to me and give me hope for life and peace with God, but I just couldn't grasp it. Things acted just like the weeds in Jesus' parable as they choked out my ability to truly receive the Word and live.

Everything in my life was plowed up and almost totally devastated before I finally received the seed of the Word in soil that was ready. God's saints were right there when this happened. I was in a place where His people were present to pick out the rocks, pull the weeds, and water as needed. The seed of the Word could finally grow and bear fruit. God patiently worked on me and waited through all those years. He had a plan for me that was much better than I could possibly imagine. I was no different than anyone else in this respect. Although I had been taught the truth, it didn't come alive in me and grow until God allowed the nearly constant series of disasters in my life to prepare the soil of my heart. This is how redemption comes to most of us.

Several things have become quite clear in the years since I completely surrendered my life to Jesus Christ. God is not just a character in a book. He is the all powerful, all knowing, and ever present Creator of everything. He is the absolutely sovereign Author and Source of everything that is true and good. He is, "The Beginning and The Ending." He is, "The King of kings and Lord of Lords." Everything that He says is true. All the promises He made in the Bible are true. I was still very weak for a time in my understanding of God's grace even after my full surrender to the King. A nagging fear used to haunt me that maybe I wasn't included in all His promises because of all the evil things I had thought, said, and done in my life. I mean, it was easy for me to believe that John Lindell, my mom, or some other saintly person was saved, but me? The simple fact is that every human is a sinner. The only human that has ever been born without inheriting a sin nature is Jesus of Nazareth.

Humanity fell when Adam and Eve sinned in the Garden of Eden. Every child born since then (except Jesus) has inherited a sin nature from the paternal side of their family. That's how inheritance works in a paternal system. The inheritance is passed from the fathers to the children. That's how inheritance works with the sin nature as well. That's why it's a critically important fact that Jesus was born to the <u>virgin</u> Mary. His biological Father is God. He didn't inherit the sin nature. He lived a perfect life on earth for about thirty three years. He never sinned. He never thought a bad thought. He never said a sinful word. He never did a sinful deed. He offered His Life of absolute perfection on the Roman cross that day in our place. He offered His Life in <u>my</u> place and in <u>your</u> place! He amazingly took <u>my</u> sin and <u>your</u> sin as if it was His Own burden of guilt and died in our place! Paul explained in one of his letters, "For our sake, He made Him to be sin who knew no sin, so that in Him we might become the righteousness of God" (2 Corinthians 5:21).

The tomb could not hold Jesus. He rose from the dead three days after He paid the price for our sins on the cross. The Bible explains that He is now seated next to God the Father in the heavenly throne room constantly advocating on our behalf. This amazing Gift is so awesome that it's very difficult for us to understand. It is absolutely true though.

We are at war, as we live out our Christian lives, against principalities and powers of spiritual darkness made up of the fallen angels who long ago rebelled against God. These evil spirits constantly fight against the church trying to destroy it from within and without. We have the freedom to choose obedience rather than rebellion through God's awesome gift of grace. We are truly saved by grace through faith in Jesus. We must then continue to occupy a flesh and blood body until God calls us home. Our bodies are not saved. Our spirits are saved. We are positionally justified at the moment we are redeemed, which means that we are declared "not guilty". We are declared by God to be righteous at that moment of justification based on Jesus righteousness which covers our sin. We begin a journey from this point of justification toward becoming separated from our old sinful way of life. This involves an ongoing succession of choices in which we as believers obediently live out our faith in love. Like any journey, it takes time. There are successes and failures along the way.

Our adoption by God into His family is the most critical part of our transformation. We become His children. He always remains with us while we go through the difficult growth process. He continues relentlessly to shape and form us into the Image of His Beloved Son. He never

leaves us and never forsakes us regardless of our failures. He disciplines us as our Heavenly Father. When we
fall, He picks us up, dusts us off, and sets us back on
the path. He is intimately and carefully aware of everything that happens in our thoughts, words, and actions.
He patiently prunes, hoes, and pulls the weeds from our
lives as the diligent Farmer who sowed the seeds of the
Word in the first place. God will make us fruitful through
all the things we experience. He has a perfect plan for
each of us. He majestically leads us to fulfillment of that
plan as He overcomes each of our weaknesses to make
us fruitful members of His family.

I unfortunately allowed circumstances and my own
sinful flesh to rule me for most of my life until I finally
surrendered everything in 2003. I've been on a fantastic
journey since then headed home to the One who gave
Himself to redeem me. Life hasn't been without trials
and challenges. There have been plenty of storms. You
know about many of these Troy. Jesus never told us that
there wouldn't be trouble in our lives after we surrender
to Him and join Him on this journey. He promised His
disciples that we would be hated and persecuted by the
world just as the world hated and persecuted Him.

Several of Jesus closest disciples were professional
fishermen. They were intimately acquainted with storms.
Jesus and His disciples were crossing the Sea of Galilee
one night in an open boat. Jesus was asleep in the back
of the boat when a terrific storm came up. The "Sea" of
Galilee is actually a freshwater lake that is mostly surrounded by high ground and mountains. Storms are not
uncommon there. They come up quickly and can be
violent.

The storm was so violent on this occasion that the boat was severely damaged and had started filling with water. These professional fishermen were terrified that they were going to drown. The wind was shrieking and the rain was probably indistinguishable from the driven spray. The surface of the lake was covered with huge rolling waves that undoubtedly dwarfed the boat as they threw it madly in multiple directions making it impossible for the occupants to have any sense of balance. The sound must have been astounding. The disciples were shocked when they noticed that Jesus was asleep in the back of the boat during this apparent disaster. They quickly fought their way back to Him and woke him by screaming, "Master, Master, we are perishing!" (Luke 8:24) Jesus woke up and rebuked the wind and waves. The wind immediately stopped and the lake became completely calm. The waves were gone! Jesus then asked them, "Where is your faith?" (Luke 8:25)

The disciples were justifiably terrified. They asked each other, "Who then is this, that He commands even winds and water, and they obey Him?" This was a very appropriate question. These fishermen had grown up on this lake. They knew the event they had just witnessed was physically impossible. They understood correctly that even if the wind suddenly stopped, the waves should have continued for hours. They recognized this as an awesome miracle. They began to understand the correct answer to the all important question Jesus Himself would later ask them, "Who do you say that I Am?" (Luke 9:20). This is, in fact, the most important question any human will ever answer.

The true answer is astounding. The God who designed water in the first place also presided over Noah's flood. The same God parted the Red Sea for Moses and the Israelites to cross; turned water into wine; and walked on the water on another stormy night. This same God was the One who was sleeping in the back of the boat that night. The disciples should have realized that it didn't matter what the storm looked or felt like if they had understood His True Identity. The boat simply <u>could not sink</u> with Him in it! This truth made His rebuke for their lack of faith perfectly just. I mention this event because the Master promised us storms in this life. The historic events in the bible actually did happen. They are recorded for a much more important reason than a mere archival record. These things are reported in God's Word for our benefit.

The boat in this story represents our individual lives. We'll get tossed and threatened by horrific storms as we go through life. Each born-again child of God can go through the storms with perfect confidence knowing that Jesus is in our boat with us and the boat simply can't sink with Him in it. Our eternity has already started. We're in these "claymation" bodies for a very short time. Jesus has a future prepared for each of us that we don't have the capacity to fully appreciate yet.

We'll never be able to do enough, or give enough, to pay the price of our sin and rebellion. Jesus said, "For God so loved the world, that He gave His Only Son. That whoever believes in Him will not perish, but have eternal life" (John 3:16). Jesus explained further through Paul, "if you confess with your mouth that Jesus is Lord and believe in your heart that God raised Him from the dead, you will be saved" (Romans 10:9). Through the Apostle John, He said, "If we confess our sins, He is faithful and just to forgive us our sins and to cleanse us from all unrighteousness" (1 John 1:9).

We will struggle through life with inherited rebellion that will end in irrevocable disaster unless we come to the end of ourselves and surrender to Jesus. This inherited rebellion will ultimately be consummated in eternal separation from our Creator unless it is interrupted by God's free gift of grace. Heaven is real, and so is hell. The Bible describes the eternal torment suffered in that place with combined references to excruciating fire and absolute darkness. God doesn't want us to end up there. He didn't create hell for man. He created it for the fallen angels. Man was given the choice to love God or not. Hell opened as a potential destination for man as a result of man's rebellion.

God constantly calls mankind to Himself in many different ways. Most people naturally continue in rebellion and sin as they sit on the throne of their lives making decisions and judgments without regard to The Rightful King. He only allows them to continue in rebellion because He has given each human the gift of choice. True love isn't just a feeling or an emotion. It's a decision. God wants us to choose to truly love Him. Jesus went on to say, "For God did not send His Son into the world to condemn the world, but in order that the world might be saved through Him" (John 3:17). Through the Apostle Peter, He said, "The Lord is not slow to fulfill His promise as some count slowness, but is patient toward you, not wishing that any should perish, but that all should reach repentance" (2 Peter 3:9).

God doesn't ask us to make this decision to love without a crystal clear example of what the choice to love really means. That's why He chose to be born as a human, to live a Perfect Life and then offer that Perfect Life to pay the Price for our rebellion. When we accept this truth and surrender everything to Him, He graciously takes all of our sin away and sets us free from the bondage to our inherited rebellious sin nature. We don't do anything to earn this gift. In fact, there's nothing we can do to earn salvation. To try to pay for any gift is insulting to the giver. To try to pay for This Gift is an absurd and in fact despicable blasphemy.

I finally woke up and accepted the Most Awesome of all gifts. Jesus then flooded my life with light, love, and joy that I still find staggering. If you're reading this and you have never truly come to the end of yourself, it's not too late. Stop right now! Cry out to Jesus to save you and set you free from your bondage to sin and pride. Surrender everything to Him. Confess your sin to Him acknowledging your personal rebellion. He's right there. He loves you absolutely. He wants you to live with Him forever.

I can't help wondering why I waited so long and wasted so much time on foolishness. It reminds me of something Jesus said to the Apostle Paul when he was crying out for relief in a time of weakness. Jesus said "My grace is sufficient for you, for My power is perfected in weakness" (2 Corinthians 12:9). Paul went on to celebrate his weakness because he realized the truth and majesty of God's Word. I can identify with that.

This is my story Troy. The explosion of change in my life is the result of God's grace, not my effort. Shock waves are produced when an explosion occurs that roll outward from the center of the blast in every direction. The profound impact of God's grace in my life has been like that. The resounding boom this explosion caused has echoed through every relationship and conversation I've been in since my redemption. I wanted to share this explosion of grace and some of the lessons I've learned in my journey with you so that you could gain some advantage as you live out your own story. There are large portions of my story that aren't pretty. Thanks to the awesome grace of God, however, you can still hear the reverberating echoes of my redemption. I can't wait to hear yours.

May God richly bless you!
Your brother in Christ,

David

CPSIA information can be obtained
at www.ICGtesting.com
Printed in the USA
FFOW02n1831050517
35304FF